FEMINISM AND TRADITION

Quiet Reflections on Ordination and Communion

T0327047

Feminism and Tradition

Quiet Reflections on Ordination and Communion

by

Lawrence R. Farley

ST VLADIMIR'S SEMINARY PRESS
YONKERS, NEW YORK
2012

Library of Congress Cataloging-in-Publication Data

Farley, Lawrence R.
  Feminism and tradition : quiet reflections on ordination and communion /
  by Lawrence R. Farley.
      p. cm.
  Includes bibliographical references.
  ISBN 978-0-88141-382-3
  1. Women in the Orthodox Eastern Church. 2. Feminism—Religious aspects—Orthodox
Eastern Church. 1. Orthodox Eastern Church—Doctrines. I. Title.

BX342.5.F37 2012
281.9082—dc23

                                                                2012019827

ST VLADIMIR'S SEMINARY PRESS
575 Scarsdale Road, Yonkers, NY 10707
1-800-204-2665
www.svspress.com

ISBN 978-088141-382-3

PRINTED IN THE UNITED STATES OF AMERICA

Dedicated to

three women of strength:

Donna, Rhiannon, and Magdalen

Contents

Foreword

Be you therefore perfect, even as your Father who is in heaven is perfect.

(Matthew 5:48)

With these few words, there is summed up the goal of our earthly lives, that is, to become saints. The acquisition of the Holy Spirit through our life in the Church is the means given to us to achieve this commandment of our Saviour Jesus Christ. Each one of us is a unique individual created by God's loving wisdom in His image. Every one was given his talents and that is what he will answer for at the last judgment.

For decades now, the western churches have been faced with questions on the roles each one can fulfill within the hierarchal structures of these churches. Some have already opened holy orders to women. Others have preferred the status quo. But for what reasons?

Father Lawrence Farley has brought to light the question, not based on emotions and political correctness but in the light of the Patristic wisdom of Christ's Church. Our Church, we believe is the One, Holy, Catholic and Apostolic Church. What makes it Catholic is that as Saint Vincent of Lérins affirmed: "*The Church of Christ, zealous and cautious guardian of the dogmas deposited with it, never changes any phase of them. It does not diminish them or add to them; it neither trims what seems necessary, nor grafts things superfluous; it neither gives up its own nor usurps what does not belong to it. But it devotes all its diligence to one aim: to treat tradition faithfully and wisely; to nurse and polish what from old times may have remained unshaped and unfinished; to consolidate and to strengthen what already was clear and plain; and to guard what already was confirmed and defined.*"

I pray that Father Lawrence's contribution to the ongoing discussions on the role of feminism and tradition may be a step to a better understanding by our western friends of the Apostolic Faith as preserved by the Orthodox Church of the Seven Oecumenical Councils.

   O Timothy, keep that which is committed to thy trust (1 Tim 6.20)

†Irénée
Bishop of Québec City

Another Book about Women in the Church?

W hy on earth would anyone want to read yet another book about women in the Church? That was the question asked by a friend of mine (admittedly, phrased much more politely and diplomatically). And indeed, a quick "Google" of the words, "women" and "church" turns up 302,000,000 entries, and there are no shortages of books dealing with the issue of woman's role in the Church. Why add yet another volume to the ever-growing pile, especially if it simply rehashes the same old arguments and takes a position behind the well-entrenched lines?

The answer is that too often our arguments do not seek to deal with the underlying issues. Some works offer a reconfigured version of the traditional faith, tweaked or transformed according to the new canons of feminism. Other works react to this proposed reconfiguring, often with no little defensiveness. There is much argument, but little dialogue. The feminist Goliath has appeared on the theological battlefield, and cannot now be ignored. Both sides seize their weapons and rush to the battle.

Feminism is indeed the defining issue of our time. Most universities offer courses in Women's Studies, and most of the books in the university libraries dealing with the issue of women in the Church may now be divided (like the division of history into "BC" and "AD"—or, if you like, "BCE" and "CE") into the eras "Before Feminism" and "After Feminism." The reader can tell at a glance into which era a given book falls by its basic presuppositions, and dismiss it (or not) accordingly.

This is apparent even in the canons of current linguistic usage: one cannot now describe, for example, the apostle Paul's message as "A Gospel for All Men" without getting into trouble. It is now "A Gospel for All People," or simply "A Gospel for All." The old collect in the classic Anglican Book of Common Prayer which bears the title, "A Prayer for all Conditions of men"[1] can no longer pass politically correct muster. As one scholar wrote, "Contemporary society, and with it the wider theological community, has simply outgrown [such usage]. We cannot but hear the world "man" as referring in the first instance to a male and only by a stretch, at best, as meaning *anthrōpos* (human being)."[2] Feminism is a comprehensive approach to life, and it examines now everything in our culture to see if it conforms to this new approach. In this examination and testing, church dogmas and practices are not exempt.

Further, a culture war is raging in the West, pitting liberal against conservative, and our discussion of the issue of feminism takes place in the midst of this combat zone. The war is a loud one, and seems to be taking no prisoners. We see it, in North America at least, in the debates about abortion and homosexuality, about contraception and State-sponsored childcare. Too often (it seems to this Canadian) the battle is drawn along strictly political lines, with American Democrats and Republicans lobbing slogans at one another across a great and bitter divide. This does not form the most helpful context in dealing with an issue as complex and important as that of the relationship of men with women in the church. Too much time is spent shouting, and not enough time listening. I remember a piece of advice given by a Marriage Encounter couple: that when husband and wife quarrel, they should do so holding hands as a way of keeping the disagreement from escalating. Whether or not this is good domestic advice, it is, I think, good cultural advice, in that both sides in the culture war would profit from having more respect for the good intentions of the opposing side, and from doing their best to avoid escalating the quarrel. As it is, the universal tendency is to demonize the opposing parties and their motives, and to answer before really listening.

This culture war has overtaken the Church when it thinks about issues of women, and in particular, the possibility of the ordination of women to Holy Orders, and of women receiving Holy Communion during their

---

[1] So titled/capitalized in the 1962 Canadian *Book of Common Prayer*.

[2] Peter C. Bouteneff, *Beginnings: Ancient Christian Readings of the Biblical Creation Narratives* (Grand Rapids, MI: Baker Academic Press, 2008), xiv.

menstrual period—the two issues principally dealt with in this volume. When I read the available literature, the first thing that strikes me is that both sides too often dismiss the arguments of the opposing side as stupid, thoughtless, and contemptible, as scarcely worth answering, as well as possibly coming from a heart that is not right with God. The note of defensiveness, if not outright anger, is unmistakable in many of the writings. The authors on both sides write with all the passion of one conducting a Crusade, a Holy War. This is perhaps not unexpected. We do not fight passionately for mere opinions or matters of taste, such as which baseball team is best, or whether chocolate is preferable to vanilla. We fight passionately when we feel that the truth of the Gospel is at stake, and the amount of strife testifies to the importance of the subject. But though the strife is understandable, it still remains unhelpful, if the issue is ever to approach resolution. We all need to acknowledge our opponents as fellow Christians, and only then begin to consider the many complex issues involved in something as fundamental to human nature as gender. In this present volume, I make no assumptions about the bad faith of those with whom I disagree. Culture wars notwithstanding, I hope to be read as speaking only to the issues addressed, namely, the possibility of women being ordained to Holy Orders, and the completely separate issue of women receiving Holy Communion during their menstrual periods. In the present climate, it seems that if one takes a certain position, other positions inevitably follow. Thus if one writes against the ordination of women to Holy Orders, some assume that the writer also is against their receiving Holy Communion while menstruating, opposes abortion and homosexuality, owns a gun and possibly belongs to the NRA, and opposes State-sponsored health care, and certainly votes Republican. I am delighted to resist such dichotomies, and to espouse positions from both opposing camps.

CHAPTER 1

The Cry of Feminism

The Oppression of Women

"*I*t's a man's world." This proverb, once a simple statement of fact, has become an indictment. (Cher, ever the cultural iconoclast, used it as the title for a music album, posing with a serpent and holding an apple.) And in this world, women are often oppressed. Many view the oppression as systemic, and see in the English language signs of the bondage, and the continued use of certain words as the means in which the bondage is normalized—hence the zeal for "inclusive language," and a refusal to use the term "man" or "mankind" as inclusive ones denoting both genders.

Whatever the case for inclusive language, there is no denying a certain amount of genuine negative discrimination. We see some of this in the marketplace, especially in the 1950's and 60's. In the past, society viewed certain employment opportunities as closed to women, despite their ability to perform the jobs. I remember as a child paging with large eyes through the Christmas catalogue every year, looking at the toy section. There was a plastic doctor's kit for boys, but a corresponding nurse's kit for the girls. The message was clear: only boys can be doctors. The highest medical "rung" to which girls could aspire was that of nurse—a significant limitation, given the strict hierarchy attending the medical profession, with doctors being considered as "higher" than nurses. In business as well, I remember how the so-called "glass ceiling" existed through which women could see, but never pass. My mother-in-law worked at a retail store part-time, with other women. The store manager, however, was always a man, brought in from outside, and never a woman promoted up through the retail ranks. My mother-in-law never wanted the top job, but that is not the point. Whatever the aspirations of the women workers, the Boss was always a man.

And not only was the Boss always a man in those past days, men and women doing the identical job, with identical education and training, and identical amounts of experience at the job, were often paid at differing rates of pay, with the women earning less. It was justified by saying that the man needed more money, since he was the principal support for his family, the main bread-winner, while the woman was more likely working there as a second income for her family. That was possibly true in those days (but increasingly less so now), but even then it was not the point. The system was set up to pay a worker for his work, without regard to his or her personal needs: if the worker was a parent of six children, no one said the job should pay more than if the worker were a parent of two children, or than if he were childless. The worker was paid for his task, period, and whether the pay was greatly needed or less so, was irrelevant to how much he was paid. The attempted justification of the pay inequity could not hold water.

Perhaps some of the most significant inequities have been in the realm of the relationship between husband and wife within the family. After all, one can expect to be battered by the world, to be disrespected by the rich and powerful. Even the Proverbs of Solomon reflect, without approval, this sad fact of life: "The poor must make entreaties; but the rich man answers roughly" (Prov 18.23). One may expect harsh dealing in the hard outer world. But when one comes home and shuts the door, one expects or hopes to find a place of safety and refuge. Home, as novelist Garrison Keillor writes, is a place where they are glad to see your face.

But sometimes, injustice and oppression persist even by the sacred hearth. It is here that women's voices must be listened to and their stories of pain given credence. In almost all cultures, not excluding the Christian one, men have exercised a kind of domination over women, in some countries regarding them as little more than chattel. Men had the privilege and power, and often used it to control, with little concern for the feelings of their wives. In this social hierarchy of power, male children were valued over female children. Women's lack of basic human rights in Islamic countries is well known, and need not be rehearsed here. Our concern, as Christians, is to throw the harsh spotlight of truth upon our own sins. As the Lord said, "To whom much is given, from him much will be required" (Lk 12.48), and we must answer to God for what we have done with the truth He has revealed to us. And the reality is that too often, we have not done very well.

Too many men have distorted the Christian teaching about the husband being the head of his wife into a licence for tyranny, forgetting that St Paul wrote not only, "wives, submit to your husbands," but also, "husbands, love your wives as Christ loved the church gave Himself up for her." Accordingly, the wife has not always been able to express herself freely, or had her counsel given due weight. Husbands, being physically stronger, and in control of the family finances, could inflict violence upon their wives with relative impunity. The suggestion that the phrase "rule of thumb" had its origin in the notion that a man could beat his wife with a stick provided it was no thicker than his thumb is, in fact, spurious.[1] But that does not invalidate the observation that wife-beating occurs, and that husbands can impose an emotional/physical tyranny over wives more than wives can over their husbands. We observe a need for Women's Shelters, not Men's Shelters.

One component in this control of women by their husbands, especially prior to the 1960s, was the presence of dependent children. An active sex life usually meant a large family, with the woman often pregnant—especially in the absence of reliable birth control until this last century. Simply put, women were more vulnerable than their husbands not only because of their pregnant state, but also because of their responsibility to feed and care for the children. The husband could roam free; the wife was often tied to the homestead. It is this fact that has made birth control (and abortion, now used as a form of retroactive birth control), a major plank in the feminist platform in their bid to achieve more freedom for women. To speak against birth control or abortion, in the view of some women, is to risk sacrificing all the gains women have made and to jeopardize their

---

[1] See Christina Hoff Sommers, *Who Stole Feminism?* (New York, NY: Simon and Schuster, 1994), 203f.

freedom. In this view, "control over our own bodies" (as the slogan has it) is necessary for retaining social freedom.

Violence against women takes many forms, with one of the most common being sexual abuse, especially in the work place. The abuse can be varied, ranging from unwanted physical contact to rape. It is so ingrained in our society and so expected that much of it goes unreported.

A further aspect of this regarding women as sexual objects, especially in North America, is the multi-million dollar pornography industry—of which the United States is the world's greatest consumer. Once again, there is a range, a continuum. At the "low end" (as it were) are magazines such as "Cosmopolitan," which sexualizes all man-woman relationships (to the detriment of the woman). At the more extreme end is the hardcore porn freely available online, and the sexual tourism available overseas. Common throughout this continuum is the objectification of women by men, and the complete separation of sexuality from authentic relationship. This was made worse by the sexual revolution of the 1960s, which promised that by separating sexuality from monogamous exclusivity, both partners would find freedom. Indeed, it is one of the great ironies of that sexual revolution, which sections of the Women's Movement have enthusiastically embraced, that the cultural and social protection which women enjoyed prior to that revolution has largely vanished. Streets are no longer safe for North American women at night. Many cities have "Take Back the Night" marches to protest this public danger (though less thought goes into considering how the night was lost in the first place).[2]

The Women's Movement has rightly shone the spotlight on the plight of women, and the challenges they face. But there are some problems.

The Women's Movement (or feminism, considered as overarching ideology) often portrays itself as simply a quest for justice, and expresses its demands with great moral indignation. To obtain its demands, it uses the paradigms established in the American Civil Rights Movement. That movement, demanding for American blacks (or African Americans) the right to vote and the right to a job free from the dictates of racial discrimi-

---

[2]It is reasonable to ask whether or not the night was ever safe for women out alone. My point is that the title of the march "Take Back the Night" assumes that something has changed, and that nights were, if not safe for women, at least safer than they currently are

nation, was simply a quest for justice. The oppression of the black by the white was unconscionable tyranny, plain and simple. Racial differences had nothing to do with one's ability to think and vote, or to do a certain job. Race is a real factor in human existence (that is, various races do obviously exist), but race is irrelevant to our basic humanity and to our entitlement, in a liberal democracy, to basic political rights. The American Civil Rights Movement was a (qualified) success, and its leaders such as Dr. Martin Luther King are rightly hailed as heroes. We now look back at the Civil Rights Movement as a shining example of an oppressed people's yearning for freedom.

It is for this reason that many feminists are eager to appropriate the terminology and legacy of the Civil Rights Movement to their own struggles and demands. Just as blacks in America have justly won rights and overturned previous ways of thinking, so, the argument goes, feminists are also entitled to have their demands met. Refusal of any of these demands is stigmatized as discrimination, and those refusing them are denounced as simply unenlightened bigots, as tragically backward as those who once denied the civil rights of African Americans. (The same strategy is now being used for those striving to push for gay rights, and proclaiming that homosexuality should have the same respectability as heterosexuality. Why depart from a proven winner?)

The demands of feminists are many and varied, for feminism is not a single homogenous movement, but a powerful river with many streams. Feminists hold a very wide banner, and claim the title "feminist" for a tremendously varied group. Some feminists denounce the institution of marriage as little better than legalized prostitution. Some are militant lesbians, and heavily invested in the gay rights movement. Some eschew all organized religion, while others are very religious. Some declare themselves to be wiccans. Some declare themselves Christians and are members of churches (sometimes leaders in churches), and strive to reform the Church on more feminist principles. Some simply demand equal pay for equal work, and value opportunities for advancement in the marketplace. Some women, dissenting from much of the angry rhetoric that characterizes the movement and many of its excesses, would not identify themselves as "feminist," but still sympathize with and support some of the same social goals. When speaking of feminism, it is difficult, if not impossible, to generalize.

The Women's Movement then, I suggest, is a mixed bag, containing both needed insights and alarming challenges. In this volume, I will be addressing the concerns of feminists who identify themselves as Christians, and who thereby acknowledge the Christian Scriptures as in some way authoritative and own the history of the Church as their own (albeit sometimes a little nervously and with some reserve). When I use the adjective "feminist," I will be referring to these Christians, sisters and brothers in Christ, with whose principles and agenda I nonetheless disagree. We agree that the Christian Scriptures are to be kept and used. We disagree about their interpretation. The perspectives of Wiccans, devout feminists of other religious faiths, and those who denounce Christianity as hopelessly patriarchal and corrupt this book does not address.

Christian Feminism

The feminist Christians with whom I will debate often say that God is speaking to the Church through the insights of the feminist movement, and we should "hear what the Spirit says to the churches" (compare Rev 2.7). The World Council of Churches adopted a slogan in 1968 that said, "The World Sets the Agenda," meaning, presumably, that the world reveals what tasks the Church must tackle, and that the Church must stand ready to serve. These theologians similarly assert God has spoken to the Church through the secular Women's Movement, summoning the Church to serve women by reordering its internal life and altering its long-cherished but erroneous categories. The spirit guiding the Women's Movement is the Holy Spirit, and so to resist the insights of feminism is to resist the Spirit of God. They say that God is doing a new thing, and calling His Church (some of them might say "calling Her Church") to walk in new ways, and to reinterpret and redefine the Faith. They call us to be open to these insights and redefinitions, and to allow them to replace older, more traditional categories and ways of thinking.

This call to redefine and reorder older ways of thinking focuses upon, among other things, the ordination of women, and (in those Orthodox circles where the prohibition still holds) the prohibition of women receiving Holy Communion while menstruating. The call to redefine is made very forcefully because, for these feminist theologians, these are matters of justice. Women have suffered injustice in being denied ordination and Holy Communion, they assert, and the injustice must now be overcome.

These new theologians see the ordination of women to diaconate, priesthood, and episcopate as simply a matter of common sense. Older generations balked at the thought of women voters, of women doctors, of women CEOs, and we have now come to see there is no reason why women may not fulfill these roles. Balking at the idea of women clergy, they argue, is simply another instance of this outdated and senseless attitude.

Some of these Orthodox theologians, like Eva Catafygiotu Topping, think that there is no reason not to ordain women to Holy Orders, since "Christ challenged outworn creeds, laws and rituals."[3] In her reconstruction of Church history, "by the end of the second century,"[4] the Fathers had altered Christ's original "liberating vision of *philanthropia* and *diakonia*"[5] so that "the days of the egalitarian church had ended" and "reaction against women's freedom and equality succeeded in limiting the royal priesthood of Eve's Christian daughters."[6] So it is that even St John Chrysostom "believed in male superiority and supremacy, in female inferiority and subservience," because he and the other Fathers were "men of their times, unable to transcend the mind-set of patriarchy, the prejudices against women."[7] (I note in passing that the admission that modern feminist theologians might be women of *their* times, unable to transcend the spirit of their *own* age, is rarely granted.) For theologians like Topping, the reordering of church practice to allow the ordination of women is the correction of a very old injustice, long in need of correction.

The same desire for the ordination of women as a matter of justice is found in Elisabeth Behr-Sigel, though offered with less stridency. She

[3]Eva Topping, *Holy Mothers of Orthodoxy* (Minneapolis, MN: Light and Life Publishing, 1987), 119.

[4]Ibid., 104

[5]Ibid., 119.

[6]Ibid., 104.

[7]Ibid., 110.

offers her reflections with greater tentativeness, with more question marks (as it were) and fewer exclamation points. Nonetheless, she also speaks from within the tradition of the Church following the World's Agenda (as the W.C.C. slogan had it), when she speaks of "the Women's Movement" as "a sign of our times" and as "a sign of that secret and irresistible force of the Spirit that is lifting humanity toward the Kingdom of the life-giving Trinity."[8] She clearly finds difficult the prohibition against women teaching in 1 Timothy 2, which she describes as "rabbinic exegesis,"[9] and the Pauline text 1 Corinthians 11.3–15 is similarly deemed "an obscure text."[10] Behr-Sigel seems uncomfortable as she grapples with these aspects of Paul's teaching, and opposes them to his assertions of reciprocity between men and women, like that found in 1 Corinthians 11.11–12. This last text she views as the preferred, true and abiding teaching of the apostle: "We see [in this text] how the Spirit clears a new path through the thick forest of human prejudices!"[11] Behr-Sigel views Paul's teaching as essentially self-contradictory, as showing an "ambivalence due to the tension between the already anticipated vision of the Kingdom and the necessary adaptation of the Gospel to specific historical and cultural settings."[12] The Fathers similarly shared "the same tensions and discontinuities"[13] as St Paul. At the end of the day, she envisions "a disciplinary pluralism"[14] in which at least some Orthodox churches will take the bold stand of ordaining women, and this ordination is clearly her hope. In her view, the present situation remains unjust, being "a society in which the feminine difference is seen as an inferiority," where "men have their place . . . always at the top

---

[8]Elisabeth Behr-Sigel, *The Ministry of Women in the Church* (Redondo Beach, CA.: Oakwood Publications, 1991), 106, 107.

[9]Ibid., 72. This discomfort with St Paul's teaching was shared by Paul Evdokimov, who in his *Woman and the Salvation of the World* (Crestwood: St Vladimir's Seminary Press, 1994) wrote (170), "Many scriptural passages [about women] . . . create an impression of scorn, sometimes even of hostility bordering on hatred, toward an impure, even demonic being. Even St Paul, steeped in rabbinic wisdom, seems to give in to this tradition when he demands the total submission of woman (Eph 5.22–24)."

[10]Ibid., 67.

[11]Ibid., 152.

[12]Ibid., 151–2.

[13]Ibid., 153.

[14]Ibid., 179.

of the pyramid of powers. As for women, their place is at the base of the pyramid . . . below the place occupied by men."[15] The injustice can only be remedied by the ordination of women.

I have looked at some length at the words of these two theologians, different as they are, because they are both Orthodox and, despite their divergence of approach, they represent a unity of agenda. Many more theologians could be cited. Their work is thoughtful and passionately argued. They all share a desire to insist on the ordination of women as a spiritual justice issue, and regard the Holy Spirit as working through the Women's Movement to bring this about. As Behr-Sigel has said, this spirit is "an irresistible force."

However, there are other spirits also active in the world besides the Holy Spirit (compare 2 Cor 11.4, 1 Jn 4.1). How does a Christian go about sorting out what is valuable in the Women's Movement from what is not, what is a genuine insight from what is a distortion?[16]

Traditionally, the Church has turned to its Scriptures to discern good from bad, and the Christian feminist theologians themselves appeal to the Scriptures. It is to some of those texts which we must now turn.

---

[15]Ibid., 149.

[16]Cf. Deborah (Malacky) Belonick, *Feminism in Christianity: An Orthodox Christian Perspective* (Sysosset, NY: Department of Religious Education, Orthodox Church in America, 1983; second edition: Yonkers, NY: St Vladimir's Seminary Press, 2012); a seminal work that compares and contrasts feminist theology with traditional Orthodox Christian theology.

CHAPTER 2

The Teaching of the Scriptures

The Authority of Scripture

Given the importance of the Scriptures for the Fathers and Orthodox Tradition generally, we will examine them at great length. But before this, I think it important to examine the concept of the authority of Scripture itself. There is a great gulf fixed between those who accept this authority and approach the Scriptures desiring to be taught and have the presuppositions inherited from this age corrected, and those resisting such correction, who approach the Scriptures prepared to reject their teaching if it is perceived that they contradict the "insights" of the modern age. I realize that in making this distinction there is a risk of stigmatization for making an *ad hominem* argument, but such a distinction is crucial nonetheless, because I believe it lies at the root of much of the feminist approach.

St Paul teaches that the Law (i.e., the Jewish Scriptures, and by extension the entire Christian Bible) is "spiritual," while we are "fleshly, sold under sin" (Rom 7.14). That means that we must approach the Scriptures as we approach no other texts, with humility and teachable hearts. Reading the Scriptures is not simply an academic or intellectual exercise (such as reading another Ancient Near Eastern text like the *Epic of Gilgamesh*), but requires the help of the Holy Spirit. St Paul said the same thing regarding the acceptance of his gospel message: "Now we have received . . . the Spirit of God . . . that we might know the things freely given to us by God . . . but the natural man does not accept the things of the Spirit of God, for they are foolishness to him, and he cannot understand them, because they are spiritually appraised" (1 Cor 2.12, 14). That is, it is only as God aids us by His Holy Spirit that we can declare "Jesus is Lord" (1 Cor 12.3), that we can accept and understand the teaching of the apostles. Thus, God's help is required to truly understand the depth of Scriptural teaching, to fully assimilate its inner meaning.

This was behind the protest of Tertullian. In his work *The Prescription against Heretics* (translated also as *"The Demurrer against the Heretics"*), the feisty North African writer argues that the heretics have no right to use the Scriptures of the Christians, since they have separated themselves from the Christian Church. The title, while savouring of a legal context, also arises from the insight that a heretic, not having the Holy Spirit, cannot but misinterpret the Holy Scriptures, since he has not "received the Spirit of God," and, being merely a "natural man," cannot "accept the things of the Spirit of God" and "cannot understand them because they are spiritually appraised."

Thus, I suggest, we need help from God, reading the Scriptures as "the things of the Spirit of God." And this help is given if we humble ourselves, seeking to be taught and corrected. It is as the prophet Isaiah said long ago: "This is the one to whom I will look—he that is humble, and contrite in spirit, and trembles at My Word" (Is 66.2). If we assume that the Scriptures are like any other ancient Near Eastern set of texts, not a living body of truth, but a literary corpse to be dissected with the scalpels of source criticism, and if we approach those texts as judges, God will not look to us, nor give us His Holy Spirit to enter into the Scriptures' inner meaning, whatever may be our valid insights and conclusions. Though we may profit by the insights of source criticism and other modern scholarly tools, at the end of the day, we must also kneel before God's Word and allow *it* to deconstruct *us*. We come to the Scriptures as disciples to be taught and corrected, not as judges to give our own verdict as to their truth.

This was the approach of the Fathers. Concerning the authority of the Scriptures, for all their diversity, the Fathers spoke with one voice. We choose but a few examples. We may quote from St Justin Martyr: "[That the Scriptures contradict each other]—I will not have the effrontery to suppose such a thing. If a Scripture which appears to be of such a kind be brought forward, since I am totally convinced that no Scripture is contradictory to another, I shall admit instead that I do not understand what is spoken of."[1] Or consider the approach of St Augustine, who takes the same attitude: "I have learned to hold those books alone of the Scriptures that are now called canonical in such reverence and honour that I do most firmly believe that none of their authors has erred in anything that he has written therein. If I find anything in those writings which seems to be contrary to the truth, I presume that either the codex is inaccurate, or the translator has not followed what was said, or I have not properly understood it."[2] Or we may quote from St Irenaeus: "[. . . We know] full well that the Scriptures are certainly perfect, since they were spoken by the Word of God and by His Spirit."[3] In all of these examples, we see a willingness to lay down one's own opinion and view and to prefer instead the teaching of the Scriptures. These are men who trembled before the Word of God.

One who stands outside the patristic mindset may well regard the Fathers' approach as outdated, since it is "pre-critical," and regard adherence to their approach as mere fundamentalism. But those who have rubbed shoulders with real fundamentalists can discern a difference between the approach of the fundamentalists and that of the Fathers. No doubt someone standing on the non-patristic side of the abyss mentioned above will be unable to discern any difference. Antipathy always blinds one to distinctions. Thus Bishop John Spong writes a book titled *Rescuing the Bible from Fundamentalism*, when he could equally have titled it, *Rescuing the Bible from Those who Believe It*, for it is not simply fundamentalism he rejects, but also any recourse to an authoritative text which might contradict the spirit of the age. Bishop Spong cannot discern any difference between fundamentalism and faith. It is easy to set up and knock down fundamentalist straw men, but more helpful is the ability to differentiate fundamentalism from the faith of the Fathers. We rightly reject fundamentalism and embrace genuine modern insights, since the critical insights of the last one hundred years do not invalidate the patristic approach, but rather can enrich it.

The abyss of which I spoke therefore does not divide the ancients from the moderns, nor "pre-critical" readers from "critical." I am not preferring

---

[1] *Dialogue with Trypho*, c. 65.
[2] Letter 82, to Jerome.
[3] *Against Heresies* 2,28,6.

the ancient "pre-critical" Fathers to modern scholars, for there are modern scholars who delight to use the insights and tools of modern critical scholarship and who nonetheless stand and work on the patristic side of this divide, reverencing and trembling before the Scriptures as the Word of God. The dividing line of which I speak does not run across the steps of the Academy, but through the human heart, whether those hearts work within the Academy or not. What matters is a willingness to allow the Scriptures to correct the spirit of the age.

The Creation Stories

It is important first to examine the creation stories in Genesis, since the New Testament (and especially St Paul) builds much of its teaching on these stories. The early chapters of Genesis contain two creation stories, which are different and complementary. This bifurcated understanding of the early chapters holds whether one subscribes to Wellhausen's so-called "Documentary Hypothesis," which posits the interweaving of four different authors, J, E, P, and D, or whether one accepts the hypothesis of D.J. Wiseman and R.K. Harrison, which posits a collection of *toldoth*, or family histories. (The former, whatever its merits, always reminded me of alphabet soup.)

THE FIRST CREATION STORY:
MALE AND FEMALE IN GOD'S IMAGE AND LIKENESS

In Genesis 1.26–30, we read the following.

> [26]Then God [Hebrew=*Elohim*] said, "Let us make *adam* in our image, after our likeness. And let them have dominion over the fish of the sea and over the birds of the heavens and over the livestock and over all the earth and over every creeping thing that creeps on the earth." [27]So God created *adam* in his own image, in the image of God he created him; male and female he created them.
>
> [28]And God blessed them. And God said to them, "Be fruitful and multiply and fill the earth and subdue it and rule over the fish of the sea and over the birds of the heavens and over every living thing that

moves on the earth." [29]And God said, "Behold, I have given you every plant yielding seed that is on the face of all the earth, and every tree with seed in its fruit. You shall have them for food. [30]And to every beast of the earth and to every bird of the heavens and to everything that creeps on the earth, everything that has the breath of life, I have given every green plant for food." And it was so.

In this translation, I have transliterated the Hebrew *adam*, rather than using the English "man," to preserve the fruitful ambiguity of the original, since *adam* functions in these narratives to denote both mankind, and also an individual male. As Bouteneff says in his *Beginnings*, "*Adam* represents a brilliant play on words whose ambiguity speaks volumes in the original language."[4] (The play on words—and much of the point of the creation narratives—tends to be obscured when translation forces a choice between "man" and "adam."[5])

While a full exegesis of the passage is beyond our scope, a few points may be made.

Mankind, *adam*, consists of both male and female, with both made equally in the image and likeness of God. The question "of what does this image consist?" is a famous one, with some of the Fathers locating it in *adam's* freedom; some, his intellect, or his soul; and some Fathers distinguishing the divine *image* (which remains after sin), from the divine moral *likeness* (which can be lost after sin). For now I would like to add the suggestion that the image (Hebrew=*tselem*) refers to exercising God's authority as His vice-regent, which is worked out as they "rule over the fish of the sea, and over the birds and over the livestock and over all the earth." The same word is used to describe idols, insofar as they were visible representations of the invisible deities. In the same way, *adam* is the visible representative of the invisible God, exercising His authority, in His Name, on His earth.[6] The Fathers, however, are not wrong, for this indeed implies

---

[4]Peter Bouteneff, op. cit., 10.

[5]See also Bouteneff's excellent delineation of the translation problems in *Beginnings*, 11, 185ff.

[6]Compare B. Waltke, *Genesis, a Commentary* (Grand Rapids, MI: Zondervan, 2001), 65–66.

a likeness to God, as *adam* resembles God in His freedom, rationality, and moral uprightness.

Here we note that male and female equally share God's authority as co-rulers over the earth. We also note that this rule is connected with God's blessing (Hebrew=*berakah*) and refers to their multiplying, so that it presupposes sexuality. For we read, "God blessed them, and God said to them, 'Be fruitful and multiply and fill the earth and subdue it and rule . . .' " The sexual fruitfulness and filling the earth is here paired with their rule and authority. We therefore suggest that Genesis here gives little encouragement to see sexual differentiation as subsequent and subordinate to God's image in us. The functioning of the *imago Dei* presupposes our functioning as male and female.

THE SECOND CREATION STORY: THE CREATION OF WOMAN

In this story, we see how the collective *adam* comes to be both male and female. (This does not presuppose that prior to this *adam* was somehow androgynous and later "split" into two.) The story, found in Genesis 2.7–8, 18–25, reads as follows. Once again, we retain certain Hebrew terms to preserve plays on words that would otherwise be lost in translation.

> [7]Then Yahweh God formed the *adam* of dust from the ground [Hebrew= *adamah*] and breathed into his nostrils the breath of life, and the *adam* became a living soul. [8]And Yahweh God planted a garden in Eden, in the east, and there he put the *adam* whom he had formed . . . [18]Then Yahweh God said, "It is not good that the *adam* should be alone; I will make him a helper corresponding to him." [19]Now out of the *adamah* Yahweh God had formed every beast of the field and every bird of the heavens and brought them to the *adam* to see what he would call them. And whatever the *adam* called every living soul, that was its name. [20]The *adam* gave names to all livestock and to the birds of the heavens and to every beast of the field. But for *adam* there was not found a helper corresponding to him. [21]So Yahweh God caused a deep sleep to fall upon the *adam*, and while he slept took one of his ribs and closed up its place with flesh. [22]And the rib that Yahweh God had taken from the *adam* he made into a woman [Hebrew=*ishah*] and brought her to

the *adam*. [23]Then the *adam* said, "This at last is bone of my bones and flesh of my flesh; she shall be called Woman [Hebrew=*ishah*], because she was taken out of Man [Hebrew=*ish*]."

[24]Therefore a man shall leave his father and his mother and hold fast to his *ishah*, and they shall become one flesh. [25]And the *adam* and his *ishah* were both naked and were not ashamed.

Here we see the theme of loving subordination, complementing the previous theme of co-equal and shared authority. The *adam* was created first, directly by God, as coming from the *adamah* or ground. This origin from the ground reveals that man is bound to the earth as to his natural ecological partner, so that it is his task to till the earth and bring out its latent potential. The partnership is seen in the play on words: *adam* comes from the *adamah*. (One translator thought to convey it with the translation "the earthling" was taken from "the earth," though to my mind this savors too much of a science-fiction mother-ship to be an elegantly workable translation.) We can see *adam's* dignity, his sharing in the divine image, through the direct infusion of the divine breath, which lifts him up from the dust and calls him to communion with his Creator. This divine image was found in the *ishah* also, since she was taken from this *adam*; the fact that the *ishah* was not made, like the *adam*, directly by the hand of God from the earth and with a direct infusion of His breath does not indicate that she has less share in His image. Also, that she is made to be *adam's* "helper" does not indicate any innate inferiority, as if she were his maid or his "domestic help." The Hebrew word for "help" or "helper," *ezer*, denotes no such inferiority, and is used for God as Israel's helper (e.g., Ps 70.5).

The subordination is, however, seen in the order of creation—*adam* was made first, and *ishah* was made as a helper corresponding to him, not *vice-versa*. That is, in the narrative, she has *her* purpose derived from *him*. Also, we see that *adam* names her, even as he named the animals, and "whatever the *adam* called every living soul, that was its name." Naming in Hebrew culture was a function of authority:[7] the *adam* named the animals

---

[7]As John Walton writes in his *Ancient Near Eastern Thought and the Old Testament* (Grand Rapids, MI: Baker Academic, 2006), 88: "In the ancient world something came into existence when it was separated out as a distinct entity, given a function, and *given a name*" (emphasis mine).

because he was the one (with the *ishah*) who was to exercise authority over them. In the same way, he sovereignly names the newly-created woman, and the solemnity and lasting authority of the act is shown by the words being in poetry.[8] It is not the case, as many have said, that "sin has subjected woman to man,"[9] since that subjection was determined prior to the Fall by the act of original creation, and expressed in Adam's naming of the woman. But—and this is crucial—we see the *nature* of the authority and corresponding subordination in what he names her: *ishah*, for she was taken from *ish*. The "-*ah*" is the Hebrew feminine ending for nouns, so that *adam* pronounces her to be an exact replica of himself, with the difference that she is feminine—"bone from his bones and flesh from his flesh," unlike the animals first brought to him by Yahweh in whom he could not discern a helper corresponding to him. *Ishah* was one suitable for sharing his thoughts, his love—and his authority to rule as God's *tselem* or image. That is why she is said to be a helper "corresponding to him" (the LXX reads, "according to him," *kat' auton*). We note too that the text stresses that *adam* had no active part in the creation of his helper, for God caused a deep sleep to fall upon him. The woman was entirely the work of God. The *adam* might have provided the "stuff" from which she was created (even as the ground provided the "stuff" for *adam*), but the *adam* could claim no part in making her. It is even possible, I tentatively suggest, to read this deep sleep as a poetic image of death, so that the text views *adam's* new life as beginning with the creation of the woman. Furthermore, the Hebrew usually translated "rib" is the Hebrew word *tsalah*, meaning "side."[10] The thought here is not of God taking a spare part from Adam which he could well do without (what's one rib, more or less?), but of taking an aspect from him, part of his very self. Thus, the subordination involved in *adam's* authority over his wife is not the subordination of an inferior to a superior, but the loving and voluntary subordination of an ontological equal.

---

[8] So rendered in all modern versions.

[9] Boris Bobrinskoy, *The Mystery of the Church: A Course in Orthodox Dogmatic Theology*, translated by Michael Breck (Yonkers, NY: St Vladimir's Seminary Press, 2011), 223.

[10] It is used in Ex 25.12 to denote the sides of the Ark of the Covenant.

THE STORY OF THE FALL

This story is found in Genesis 3.1–24 and, given its importance, may be quoted in full.

[1]Now the serpent was more cunning than any other beast of the field that Yahweh God had made.

He said to the *ishah*, "Did God actually say, 'You shall not eat of any tree in the garden'?" [2]And the *ishah* said to the serpent, "We may eat of the fruit of the trees in the garden, [3]but God said, 'You shall not eat of the fruit of the tree that is in the midst of the garden, neither shall you touch it, lest you die.'" [4]But the serpent said to the *ishah*, "You will not surely die. [5]For God [=*Elohim*] knows that when you eat of it your eyes will be opened, and you will be like gods [=*elohim*], knowing good and evil." [6]So when the *ishah* saw that the tree was good for food, and that it was a delight to the eyes, and that the tree was to be desired to make one wise, she took of its fruit and ate, and she also gave some to her *ish* who was with her, and he ate. [7] Then the eyes of both were opened, and they knew that they were naked. And they sewed fig leaves together and made themselves loincloths. [8]And they heard the sound of Yahweh God walking in the garden in the cool of the day, and the *adam* and his *ishah* hid themselves from the presence of Yahweh God among the trees of the garden. [9]But Yahweh God called to the *adam* and said to him, "Where are you?" [10]And he said, "I heard the sound of you in the garden, and I was afraid, because I was naked, and I hid myself." [11]He said, "Who told you that you were naked? Have you eaten of the tree of which I commanded you not to eat?" [12]The *adam* said, "The *ishah* whom you gave to be with me, she gave me fruit of the tree, and I ate." [13]Then Yahweh God said to *ishah*, "What is this that you have done?" The *ishah* said, "The serpent deceived me, and I ate."

[14]Yahweh God said to the serpent, "Because you have done this, cursed are you above all livestock and above all beasts of the field; on your belly you shall go, and dust you shall eat all the days of your life. [15]I will put enmity between you and the *ishah*, and between your offspring and her offspring; he shall bruise your head, and you shall bruise his heel."

¹⁶To the *ishah* he said, "I will surely multiply your pain in child-bearing; in pain you shall bring forth children. Your desire shall be for your *ish*, and he shall rule over you."

¹⁷And to *adam* he said, "Because you have listened to the voice of your *ishah* and have eaten of the tree of which I commanded you, 'You shall not eat of it,' cursed is the ground [=*adamah*] because of you; in pain you shall eat of it all the days of your life; ¹⁸thorns and thistles it shall bring forth for you; and you shall eat the plants of the field. ¹⁹By the sweat of your face you shall eat bread, till you return to the ground [=*adamah*], for out of it you were taken; for you are dust, and to dust you shall return."

²⁰The *adam* called his *ishah's* name Eve [Hebrew=*Chavvah*], because she was the mother of all living [Hebrew=*chay*]. ²¹And Yahweh God made for *adam* and for his *ishah* garments of skins and clothed them.

²²Then Yahweh God said, "Behold, the *adam* has become like one of us in knowing good and evil. Now, lest he reach out his hand and take also of the tree of life and eat, and live forever—²³therefore Yahweh God sent him out from the garden of Eden to work the ground [=*adamah*] from which he was taken. ²⁴He drove out the *adam*, and at the east of the garden of Eden he placed the cherubim and a flaming sword that turned every way to guard the way to the tree of life.

We see in the text that once again solemn pronouncements of lasting import are given as poetry. A full exegesis of the text is beyond our scope, but I would make several observations. First, the serpent appeals to the woman as the more vulnerable. For whatever reason, his strategy works, and the woman is deceived. Also, the man "who was with her" followed her lead and ate also. Whether the man was deceived or not, the text does not say, but the emphasis is on the woman's deception and the husband's obedience to the woman; there is no suggestion that he also "saw the fruit was to be desired to make one wise." Further, the immediate result of their joint disobedience was shame with each other, and alienation from God. (We note that the result is shame at nakedness, not the beginning of sexuality.) I would suggest that although all three are blamed and are punished with a judgment from God, the bulk of the blame falls on the man. He is the leader (he names the woman, and not *vice-versa*), and as the head, carries the ultimate responsibility. Also, since there is no indication that the man was deceived by the serpent, this means that he sinned with a greater knowledge of wrongdoing. (It is perhaps for this reason that St Paul declares that death enters through the man Adam, and not the woman.) While it is true that the woman led the man into sin, the fact that she had been genuinely deceived means that the bulk of the responsibility lies with the man.

We must now look more closely at the specific words of judgment directed at the man and the woman, and see how each one is tailored to their respective vocations. Both inherit death (seen in the later expulsion from access to the tree of life), but before this expulsion, individual and differing judgments are pronounced on each of them. The woman's vocation is to be life-bearer, to bring forth children. Now she must fulfill that vocation with multiplied pain (Hebrew=*etsev*). Moreover, her "desire will be for her husband, and he will rule over her." What is this about?

The word translated "desire" is the Hebrew *teshuqah*, indicating longing. In response to this desire, the husband will "rule" her (Hebrew= *mashal,* a different word than *radah*, the one used in Gen 1.28). The word *mashal* is variously used in the Old Testament, and need not necessarily imply enforced servility; it is used for the beneficent ruling of the sun and moon over the day and the night in Genesis 1.18. What is the nature of this desire for and subsequent rule by the husband? A clue may be found in comparing the judgment on the man.

The man's vocation is to "till the [the garden of Eden] and keep it" (Gen 2.15), for up until then "there was no *adam* to till the *adamah*" (2.5). He must now fulfill that vocation with pain (Hebrew=*etsev*; the same word used to describe the woman's pain as she fulfills her vocation), in that the *adamah* is cursed and will now bring forth thorns and thistles. The task that was to be easy and joyful is now hard and painful, and man will know his weakness as he labors and eats the resultant food "by the sweat of his face." The serpent had promised that disobedience would bring strength so that they would be as gods (=*elohim*), but it had brought only weakness, leading to death. The common theme of pain (Hebrew=*etsev*) is used to describe both the man and woman as they fulfill their original vocations, and this pain witnesses to their weakened condition. Accordingly, I suggest that the woman's desire for her *ish* is not a sexual desire, but a desire for protection brought on by her new weakness, and consequently his "rule" over her is that of a dominion of protection in a now hostile world. Note: the disobedience and fall do not produce the element of subordination in their relationship,[11] for that was present prior to fall, as we saw in *adam's* naming of his *ishah*. This new element of rule witnesses to her new need for protection and her new weakness. This understanding finds some support in the LXX version, which reads that "your turning (Greek= *apostrophē*) shall be to your husband," as the woman turns to him for support and protection.

At the end of the story, as the couple leaves the Garden to begin their long exile in the outer world, we see that the *adam* again names his wife. He had once made the pronouncement, "She shall be called *ishah*, because she was taken out of *ish*," and now he gives her another name, naming her "*Chavvah*," because she is mother of all the living (Hebrew=*chay*). It is another play on words, and one that vanishes once it is translated into English, with "Eve" being the mother of all the "living." (The play on words is retained in the LXX Greek—though at the cost of changing her name from *Chavvah* into *Zoe*, so that she could be seen as the mother of all the *zōntōn*.) This second naming is significant. Originally the man had declared the woman's significance vis-à-vis himself, that she was "his other half," his soul-mate, a helper corresponding to his nature, flesh of his flesh. The first naming was an act of delight, of discovery of the woman as God's gift to him. Now, in this second naming, he declares her significance not just as relating to himself, but to their entire world. As they face a life outside the protection of the Garden, far from repudiating her for her role in their catastrophe, he exalts her, bestowing a name that reveals her destiny: she is to be the mother of all who live. In this he reflects the grace of God, who cared for the man and the woman after their fall by clothing them with skins for warmth.[12] As one writer said, "Adam names the

---

[11]Though this was the interpretation of St John Chrysostom; compare his Homily 9 on 1 Timothy.

[12]Compare the observation of Victor Hamilton in his commentary *Genesis, Chapters*

woman 'Life', lifting her above all else, including himself."[13] This second naming, though an expression of the man's authority, redounds to the honor of the woman. Even in the world of exile, the woman retains the glory due her role.

In summary, we see in these Genesis narratives what was then a revolutionary view of human nature. Indeed, the entire creation narrative can be read as a kind of protest against the culture of its time. In the ancient pagan world, only the king was said to be "in the image of God,"[14] but here we find all human beings adorned with that image. In ancient thought, realities such as music, animal husbandry, and metallurgy were the gifts of the gods, but in Genesis they are portrayed as human accomplishments (Gen 4.20–22). All of this radically differentiated the people of Israel from their pagan neighbors, and witnessed to their God as a God who invests in humanity's freedom and dignity. In that ancient world, women were little more than chattel (as seen in polygamy as a source of status), but here the woman jointly shares the authority with the man as God's image in the world. We also see subordination of the wife to the husband, but the subordination is the loving and voluntary subordination of an ontological equal, as they rule together in unity. The authority of the man over his wife does not detract from her dignity. Even after their calamitous fall, their high dignity remains as those cared for by God, and their names witness to this: he is "Mankind"; she is "Life."

The Teaching of Christ

Christ's teaching on men and women must be located in His overall teaching about the Kingdom of God. The Kingdom of God, as it broke in upon Israel and the world, called all to freedom and love; it called all to part with past ways, and to receive God's grace, even if that new wine broke apart the old wineskins of religion (compare Mk 2.22). Old approaches to prayer, almsgiving, and fasting were to be reconsidered (Mt 6.1ff; Mk 2.18–20),

---

1–17 (Grand Rapids, MI: Eerdmans, 1990), 207: "Just as Adam renames his spouse, so God reclothes the couple themselves."

[13]Brook Herbert, "Towards the Recovery of a Theology of Patriarchy," in *Saint Vladimir's Theological Quarterly* 40.4 (1996): 297.

[14]B. Waltke, op. cit., 66.

and even old approaches to the Sabbath (Mk 2.23–27). Thus Christ healed Gentiles, and was even willing to enter their homes, despite the certainty of contracting ceremonial defilement (Lk 7.1). He was willing to eat with tax-collectors and notorious sinners, regardless of their past (Lk 7.36f, 15.2). All that mattered was coming to God with a humble heart, accepting His invitation to enter the Kingdom, with a readiness to change.

His dealings with women were characterized by the same openness and willingness to trample upon old prejudices. Unlike the Rabbis (some of whom said it were better for the Torah to be burnt than be taught to a woman[15]), He received women as disciples as freely as He received men. Thus when His friend Mary outraged all decent custom by leaving her sister to prepare the meal for the Christ and His men while she sat down among them and listened to His teaching, He defended her action, saying that she had chosen the one thing needful (Lk 10.38f). Gender was no barrier to discipleship. He even allowed women to follow Him about the land with other disciples (Lk 8.1–3). We note, however, whatever its significance and rationale, that Jesus chose no woman to be part of the authoritative Twelve (or, so far as we know, of the Seventy). Given His complete acceptance of women as disciples and His willingness to defy Jewish cultural precedent if such precedents went contrary to the new norms of the Kingdom, it is difficult to imagine that the absence of women from these positions of authority is without significance.[16]

For Jesus, the Law's true and original intent is to be fulfilled now that the Kingdom has come. Thus, for example, God's original intent was for people to live in love, so that the commandment of the Law accordingly said, "You shall not murder" (Ex 20.13). But now that the Kingdom had come (and with it the Holy Spirit, whose power was able to transform human nature and empower people to do what was previously impossible; Jn 7.37–39, Mt 19.26), a newer and higher standard was demanded. The underlying intent and final aim of the commandment not to murder was

[15]Compare the saying ascribed to Rabbi Eleazar in the Talmud in Sotah 3:4, "I would rather have the roll of the Law burnt than have it taught to a woman."

[16]Compare Manfred Hauke, who speaks of "the will of Christ as the crucial reference point," and as expressed in "the behavior of Jesus, who called no women to apostolic service although he could also have acted differently" (*Women in the Priesthood?* [San Francisco: Ignatius Press, 1988], 435, 437).

now to be fulfilled: people were not only to avoid outward murder, but also inward hatred (Mt 5.21–22).

We can also see this element of restoration, and returning to God's original and pristine intent, in Christ's teaching on divorce. In the Rabbinical interpretations of His time, divorce was allowed, since a provision of the Law allowed a man to divorce his wife if he "finds some indecency in her" (Deut 24.1). The Rabbis seized on this provision and debated what "some indecency" might mean—did it mean adultery, or anything that displeased the husband? (Not surprisingly, the latter interpretation was the more popular.) But Christ did not concern Himself to decide which of the two interpretations was correct. Now that the Kingdom had come, His disciples were called to a higher standard (much to the initial astonishment of the Twelve; see Mt 19.10). That is, He said that such a provision had been allowed Israel only "because of their hardness of heart" (Mt 19.8), but He referred His disciples back to the original intent of the Law, expressed most clearly in the creation stories. "From the beginning," Christ said, "He made them male and female," and when the man is "joined to his wife," "the two shall become one flesh" (Mt 19.4–5). God made the two into one, but divorce would divide what God had united and work against the intention of God. So, divorce was now altogether disallowed.

We see that Christ did not set aside the Law, but appealed to its original intention. A Pharisaical reliance upon the Law for righteousness was set aside, by Christ and equally by His chosen vessel, St Paul. But the original intent of the Law was not set aside, but brought forward as the restored norm. It is thus wrong to oppose Christ and the Law, or St Paul and the Law. The real situation is more nuanced. What Christ (and St Paul) opposed and set aside as belonging to the old age was *the Law as religion*, the Law as the basis of one's approach to God. Christ appealed to the original intent of the Law when He opposed the teaching of the creation stories to the provision allowed in Deuteronomy. St Paul appealed to the original intent of the Law when he said that "Love is the fullness of the Law" (Rom 13.10), and, "Do we overthrow the Law by this faith? By no means! On the contrary, we uphold the Law" (Rom 3.31). For Christ (as for Paul), the Law, when correctly read, reveals the basis for the interactions of man and woman, husband and wife.

The Teaching of St Paul

St Paul's teaching is always occasional. That is, he never sets out his views and teachings in neat packages in a kind of Systematic Theology. Rather, he writes as a pastor to communities he loves, and strives to help them conform their lives to the higher standard of the Gospel. Thus, his teaching on men and women has to be distilled from several of his epistles. We will look at his epistles to the Corinthians, the Ephesians, the Galatians, and Timothy. The Pauline authorship of all of these has been disputed (especially his authorship of the Pastorals), but for a Christian, the authority of the books of the New Testament does not stand or fall with questions of authorship. We will therefore leave such questions to one side. In our examination of the Pauline texts below, we will also note the feminist interpretations of some Orthodox writers, since we offer our view as an alternative. No attempt will be made to be exhaustive, but certain texts will be chosen as representative of Paul's thought.

THE TEACHING OF ST PAUL: 1 CORINTHIANS 11

In the passage in 1 Corinthians 11.2–16, we see Paul writing to correct an incipient problem in Corinth. Paul's teaching had been wildly misunderstood in that city. When he had said, "All things are lawful for me" (see 1 Cor 6.12), they assumed that this included fornication as well (since fornication was, after all, something of a civic tradition in Corinth), and Paul had write to clear up this misunderstanding. It was the same with his approach to freedom in Christ. He had taught them that men and women were equal in Christ's salvation (cf. Gal 3.28), and some women in Corinth assumed that this meant that gender distinctions were no longer valid. Accordingly, they were contemplating removing their head-covering, since in that culture the head-covering was the most visible sign of their gender specificity (to use today's jargon) and of their submission to their husbands.[17] Not only would this visually stunning renunciation of

---

[17]E. Schüssler Fiorenza suggests that the problem was not dispensing with head-covering, but of unbinding the hair during worship, arguing from v. 15, which says that a woman's hair is given for a covering. *In Memory of Her* (New York, NY: Crossroad Publishing, 1990), 228. Few should follow such an idiosyncratic reading, since Paul speaks of the women

the husband's leadership bring bad press to the Christians by suggesting they promoted domestic anarchy, it would also be contrary to the internal principles of life in Christ. So, Paul does not simply forbid the Corinthian women to discard their head-coverings, and say that no offense must be given to outsiders. In fact, the "give no offense to outsiders" argument, though used by Paul in teaching about food offered to idols (1 Cor 10.32–33), is not mentioned in his teaching about women's head-coverings at all. Rather, he begins a long argument to show why such a move would violate the Christian understanding of man-woman relationships, which he says forms part of "the traditions," the original apostolic deposit which he "delivered to" them (1 Cor 11.2). In promoting these "traditions," he argues from Scripture (i.e., the Old Testament), from nature, and from universal church practice.

We give the part of Paul's argument from the Old Testament creation stories in full, as found in 1 Corinthians 11.3–12, leaving to one side his arguments from nature (v. 13–15), and from universal church practice (v. 16). The translation used is that of the English Standard Version, which mostly translates the Greek *gynē* as "wife," rather than "woman." This is reasonable, since Paul was dealing with relationships between husband and wife, and not with women and men *per se*. Paul is not subordinating all women to all men, nor suggesting that a woman must be in submission to a man somewhere, so that an adult woman, if unmarried, must be in submission to her father in a way that an adult son is not. Paul is not thinking here of single women and their situation at all, and it is illegitimate for an expositor to wrench the teaching here from its original context. (See the brief excursus below.)

> [3]But I want you to understand that the head of every man is Christ, the head of a wife is her husband, and the head of Christ is God. [4]Every man who prays or prophesies with his head covered dishonors his head, [5]but every wife who prays or prophesies with her head uncovered dishonors her head, since it is the same as if her head were shaven.

being required to have "authority on their head"—i.e., a veil, the symbol of authority (so RSV). Note: Paul's direction was to put something *over* the hair, not to simply "keep their hair bound up."

[6]For if a wife will not cover her head, then she should cut her hair short. But since it is disgraceful for a wife to cut off her hair or shave her head, let her cover her head. [7]For a man ought not to cover his head, since he is the image and glory of God, but woman is the glory of man. [8]For man was not made from woman, but woman from man. [9]Neither was man created for woman, but woman for man. [10]That is why a wife ought to have a symbol of authority on her head, because of the angels. [11]Nevertheless, in the Lord woman is not independent of man nor man of woman; [12]for as woman was made from man, so man is now born of woman. And all things are from God.

In his discussion of the propriety of women covering their heads, Paul regards the issue as having to do with relationships and authority (this allows a play on words, since "head" (Greek=*kephalē*) means both the physical head on one's shoulders and also one's spiritual leader. For him, the problem with a wife uncovering her physical head is that it involves renouncing her submission to her spiritual head, her husband. The scandal of this would have been seen by society at large at that time. In this passage, there are, sadly, a number of questions that cannot be answered with confidence. Was Paul speaking of women uncovering their heads at all times when in public, or only during Christian worship? And granted that adult Jewish women covered their heads in public, did the same apply to women in Greco-Roman cities? Despite the assertions of some commentators, certainty about these things still eludes us.[18] Fortunately the answers to these questions are not crucial to the concerns dealt with in this study.

Paul begins by focusing on the central part of the tradition he delivered to them—namely, that women must abide in the divine order in which their husbands and even Christ have their own place. Men have Christ as their head, and are responsible to him, even as Christ has God (i.e., the Father) as His head and is responsible to Him. Given this, the woman's act of repudiating her husband's headship is revealed as violation of divine order, especially repugnant during worship.[19] Their men and even Christ

[18]Compare Stephen B. Clark's *Man and Woman in Christ* (Ann Arbor, MI: Servant Books, 1980), 168–169.

[19]Paul's reference in v. 10 about the necessity of a head-covering "because of the angels"

remains in submission: why don't they? In speaking of Christ being the head of the man and God being the head of Christ, it is important not to press Paul's words beyond his immediate intention. Paul is not suggesting some sort of chain of command, as if the wife could only reach Christ through the husband. His sole point is that everyone is responsible to someone, and this includes the women. We must also be clear that in insisting on the wife's subordination to her husband, Paul does not thereby declare her inferior to him. Subordination does not imply inferiority. This can be deduced from the very examples Paul offers: Christ is subordinate to God the Father, yet He is equal to Him ontologically. The essential inferiority of women to men has no place in the thought of St Paul.

Then comes a series of observations: if a man covers his head during worship, it would be dishonoring, but if a woman *un*covers her head during worship, it would be dishonoring—just as dishonoring as it would be for her to have her head shaved. Curtly, Paul challenges the women: if you would uncover your head, then go all the way and cut off your hair! But since you would never do this, then cover your head. You must take your pick! Paul then argues from the creation stories, and it seems as if many feminist authors find his argument difficult to stomach. One writer describes the reasoning "as subtle as it is obscure," as a "thick forest of human prejudices"[20] Another speaks of a "very convoluted argument, which can no longer be unraveled completely"[21] This is not favorite feminist reading.

In Paul's understanding of the creation stories, man has a primordial preeminence that is the basis of his headship regarding his wife (and the reason why the Corinthian women must express this headship by covering their heads). Man was created as "the image and glory of God," whereas "woman is the glory of man." (Note that this does not deny that woman is also in the image of God.) What then does it mean to say that "man is the glory of God"? I suggest that Paul is referring to the actual creation account in Genesis 2.7, and that man is "God's glory" in the sense that he

---

probably refers to this, since the angels were present at Christian worship as guardians of divine order in the world.

[20]E. Behr-Sigel, op. cit., 152.

[21]E. Schüssler Fiorenza, op. cit., 228.

brings glory to God, revealing how glorious God is to have created such a one in His image from the mere dust of the earth. If this is a correct interpretation, we see also in what sense "woman is the glory of man"—that she brings glory to him, since in Genesis 2.21–22 she was created for him (and not *vice-versa*), and her created splendor redounds upon him. Thus one commentator says, "Man reveals how beautiful a being God could create . . . a woman reveals how beautiful a being God could create from a man."[22] Such an understanding finds an echo in Proverbs 11.16, which in the LXX reads, "A gracious wife brings glory to her husband, but a woman hating righteousness is a throne of dishonor." Thus, Paul argues, man is to glorify his head, Christ, and the woman is to glorify her head, the husband, both by acting in such a way as not to disgrace.

Then, in 1 Corinthians 11.8–9 we find Paul's interpretation of the creation of Eve from Adam: "man was not made from woman, but woman from man"—a clear reference to Genesis 2.21–22 (as is his "woman was made for man" in v. 12). Also, "neither was man created for woman, but woman for man." Here the temporal priority in creation witnesses to a spiritual priority and headship. Paul argues by this that Eve was created for Adam, and so the leadership belongs to him. (What this leadership entails precisely, we will see in Eph 5.)

This is followed by v. 11–12: "Nevertheless, in the Lord woman is not independent of man, nor man of woman; for as woman was made from man, so man is now born of woman. And all things are from God." Having established that woman had her origin from man in the Garden, he balances this by adding that all men now take their origin from women, their mothers. He is keen to point this out, saying that "in the Lord woman is not independent of man nor man of woman," but rather both are joined to the Lord as one flesh, and are called to mutual service.[23] The woman's ultimate focus is therefore not toward her husband, but toward Christ,

---

[22]F.W.Grosheide, *Commentary on 1 Corinthians* (Grand Rapids, MI: Eerdmans, 1953), 256.

[23]This mutual service is reflected also in Paul's teaching in 1 Cor 7.4: "the wife does not have authority over her own body, but the husband does; and likewise the husband does not have authority over his own body, but the wife does." This last assertion of the wife's authority over the husband's body radically differentiates Paul's teaching from the secular Greco-Roman views of his day.

since "all things are from God." He is the ultimate source of all life for both men and women, and the focus of all Christians must be toward Him.

Some have suggested that this balancing (as woman was from man, so now all men are from women) is not so much balancing as backtracking. One writer says that Paul here first sets a double standard and then "appears to backtrack, mitigating the absolute subordination of women to men . . . having advanced the argument of woman's derivation from man as a possible reason for the difference in headgear, he immediately *rejects* this argument*,*" since the derivation argument is a part of the Old Testament inheritance transcended "in the Lord."[24] The same writer quotes with approval Fiorenza's statement, "In the Christian community, men and women are not different from each other. Differences which might exist on the basis of nature and creation are no longer present in the worship assembly."[25]

St Paul was not in the habit of backtracking, especially when giving directions to difficult communities. He was, however, known to add a parenthesis to his words, guarding the reader from unwarranted conclusions. Thus, in 1 Corinthians 7.21ff, he argues that slave or free status is spiritually irrelevant, since a slave is freed by Christ in his heart, and the free man is bound to Christ in his heart. He writes, "Were you called as a slave? Don't worry about it," and then immediately adds in a kind of parenthesis, "But if you are able also to become free, use that"[26]—lest his readers conclude that Paul would counsel passing up the opportunity for freedom. Or take for example Paul's words in 1 Corinthians 10.28, where he teaches that one should refuse food sacrificed to idols "for conscience' sake"—he immediately adds in a parenthesis, "I mean not your own conscience, but the other's." Or take Philippians 4.10, where he writes from prison of his joy in finally receiving the money they sent him. Lest they conclude from this that he speaks from want, he immediately adds, "Not that I speak from want, for I have learned to be content in whatever circumstances I am." Or take his advice to Timothy in 1 Timothy 5.22:[27] "Keep yourself

---

[24]Bouteneff, op. cit., 47, 48, italics his.
[25]Ibid., 48, quoting Fiorenza, op. cit., 230.
[26]The translated sense of AV, RSV, NASB, NEB, TEV, Jerusalem Bible.
[27]I take the Pastorals to be Pauline.

pure from sin." Lest Timothy conclude that this purity involves a continued asceticism in drinking only water, the writer adds, "No longer drink
water only, but use a little wine for the sake of your stomach." In all these
examples, we see not backtracking, but parenthetical clarification, addi-
tions put in to avoid possible misunderstanding. I believe that is what
we find in 1 Corinthians 11.11–12—Paul is concerned lest his readers
take his insistence on a wife's subordination to her husband to overthrow
their fundamental unity and equality in Christ. "In the Lord" as married
Christians, neither one is independent (literally "without," Greek=*chōris*)
of the other, but (anticipating his teaching in the epistle to the Ephesians),
both are one flesh in Christ. Paul sees this balance as manifested in history: woman's primordial origin from Adam finds its providential balance
in all men's birth from women, and this witnesses to God as the ultimate
source of life for all.

A BRIEF NOTE ON THE SINGLE CHRISTIAN WOMAN

In his teaching in 1 Corinthians 11, St Paul assumes that the adult women
in the congregation are married, so that the Greek *gynē* can be translated
either as "woman" or "wife." In the world of the New Testament, most
women were married or widowed, as economics did not allow easily for the
survival of single women. Certain rich women may have chosen to remain
single (it appears that Lydia in Acts 16.14 was one of them, as was Olympias
the deaconess and friend of St John Chrysostom in the fourth century), but
the poor single woman was a comparative rarity. Most women married at a
young age. The author of 1 Timothy 5.3ff assumes that young widows will
remarry, and that older widows will find a home with and be cared for by
their families if they have any. It is otherwise today, with many Christian
women being single, either by choice, circumstances, or divorce. A word
therefore may be said regarding single Christian women.

The contemporary church needs to acknowledge the unique situation
of the single Christian—of both genders. It is not the case that choices for
Christians are confined to marriage or monasticism. It is possible to live a
life of obedience to Christ and remain single, though the single Christian
today has challenges of loneliness and of living alone, which challenges

may only increase with age. As Ecclesiastes 4.9–10 says, "Two are better than one . . . for if either of them falls, the one will lift up his companion. But woe to the one who falls when there is not another to lift him up!" It is all the more important for the local church community to take steps to include singles in their social events, and to exercise proper pastoral care for them in times of sickness or other distress when extra help may be required and appreciated. Paul writes in 1 Cororinthians 7.32f that the single Christian has opportunities to grow in prayer not possible for the Christian who is married with children. The single celibate life may have its distinct challenges, but the path to holiness lies more wide open. This is not because sexuality is somehow defiling (there is no hint of that in Paul), but rather because the single life provides more opportunities for solitude and prayer. This is not to suggest that celibacy in itself has no significance. Rather, the female celibate's "concern about the things of the Lord, that she may be holy both in body and spirit" (1 Cor 7.34) finds bodily expression in her celibacy, as the innermost parts of the life are reserved entirely for the Lord.

THE TEACHING OF ST PAUL: 1 CORINTHIANS 14

Elsewhere in Paul's letter to the Corinthians, he takes pains to correct abuses in the weekly Eucharistic *synaxis* (or liturgical assembly). In that gathering, many of them were speaking in tongues at the same time, so that it appeared chaotic. In chapters 12–14, Paul therefore gives them corrective counsel. In chapter 12, he first argues that the gift of tongues is but one of the gifts of the Spirit, and not even the most important one. First in importance comes the gift of apostles, then prophets, then teachers, then miracles, and only then comes the gift of tongues, the last of a longer list including healings, helps, and administrations. What matters is that all the gifts are given by God as God wills, and all the gifts have different functions, just like the members or organs of the human body. Just as God arranges the body as He wills, so He distributes spiritual gifts as He wills, and all His gifts should be valued, not just tongues. In chapter 13, Paul offers a better way than using the gifts competitively; the way of love, wherein the gifts are used to build up the common body of the faithful.

In chapter 14, he argues for the superiority of prophecy over tongues, and concludes by giving concrete pieces of advice for how Christians must conduct themselves in their gatherings. The relevant verses are 1 Corinthians 14.27–40:

> [27]If any speak in a tongue, let there be only two or at most three, and each in turn, and let someone interpret. [28]But if there is no one to interpret, let each of them keep silent in church and speak to himself and to God. [29]Let two or three prophets speak, and let the others weigh what is said. [30]If a revelation is made to another sitting there, let the first be silent. [31]For you can all prophesy one by one, so that all may learn and all be encouraged, [32]and the spirits of prophets are subject to prophets. [33]For God is not a God of confusion but of peace. As in all the churches of the saints, [34]the women should keep silent in the churches. For they are not permitted to speak, but should be in submission, as the Law also says. [35]If there is anything they desire to learn, let them ask their husbands at home. For it is shameful for a woman to speak in church. [36]Or was it from you that the word of God came? Or are you the only ones it has reached? [37]If anyone thinks that he is a prophet, or spiritual, he should acknowledge that the things I am writing to you are a command of the Lord. [38]If anyone does not recognize this, he is not recognized. [39]So, my brothers, earnestly desire to prophesy, and do not forbid speaking in tongues. [40]But all things should be done decently and in order.

Before interpreting this text, a word must be said about its integrity. Some interpreters (such as Gordon Fee[28]) understand v. 34–35 as a non-Pauline interpolation, added later by a scribe as a marginal gloss and then mistakenly incorporated into the text itself. Fee argues this from the perception that these verses contradict Paul's teaching in 1 Corinthians 11.2–16, and also from some manuscript evidence. In particular, a few Greek manuscripts and some bilingual Latin-Greek ones and other Latin ones have the verses, but place them after 1 Corinthians 14.40. This, he argues, is evidence that they are not authentic to Paul.

---

[28]Gordon Fee, *The First Epistle to the Corinthians* (Grand Rapids, MI: Eerdmans, 1987), 699–708.

On the other hand, others dispute this.[29] One can find evidence of the displacement of other New Testament verses whose Pauline authorship is undoubted. The words "and the church in their house" from Romans 16.5 is displaced to after 16.3; the words "and all the churches of Christ" from Romans 16.16 is displaced to after 16.21. The transpositions are triggered by certain words, and the dislocation of passages in these Latin-Greek manuscripts is not uncommon, and is not evidence of interpolation. Furthermore, we have repeated vocabulary in the disputed verses that is common to the rest of the passage—notably the verb *sigaō*, found also in 14.28, 30 (see exegesis below). Regarding Fee's contention that these verses contradict Paul's thought in 1 Corinthians 11.2ff, we hope to show that the teaching is substantially the same in both cases: namely, that wives must express their subordination to their husbands by their behavior in the Christian *synaxis*. One cannot help but think that scholars such as Fee are all-too-happy to eliminate unwelcome teaching from the genuine works of Paul. The Pastorals (with their unwelcome 1 Tim 2.11–12) have been successfully banished, and they jump at any opportunity to eject 1 Corinthians 14.34–35 as well. In the Greek manuscripts, we see an early and wide attestation for the usual placement of these verses—including the significant manuscript P46. Thus the text may be allowed to stand as is.

In this text, we see Paul's concern for decorum, decency, and order (v. 40). This is secured in the case of tongues by letting two or three speak in tongues, and then waiting for an interpretation. If this latter is not forthcoming, "let each keep silent (Greek=*sigatō*) in church" (v. 28), speaking in tongues not aloud, but privately to God. This decorum is secured in the case of prophecy by letting two or three prophets speak, and by waiting for "the others" to weigh what is said. If one of those "sitting" as judges receives a revelation that the prophecy is not valid, "let the first (i.e., the original prophet) be silent" (Greek=*sigatō*) (v. 30). Then come the words, "as in all the churches of the saints, the women should be silent (Greek=

[29]Jeffrey Kloha of Concordia University, St Louis, in his study, "The Displacement of 1 Corinthians 14.34–35 in D F G and the Latin Tradition." See also the discussion of Manfred Hauke in his *Women in the Priesthood?* (San Francisco: Ignatius Press, 1988), 390–394, where he locates the textual disruption in the influence of heretics such as Marcion.

sigatōsan) in the churches. They are not permitted to speak, but should be in submission, as the Law also says."

It is fair to say that a number of people have gotten a lot of mileage out of these words, even at the cost of their context and meaning. What was Paul talking about? Did he really mean that women should remain absolutely mute while in the Christian *synaxis*? If that were the case, how could they pray and prophesy, as Paul assumes they were doing in 1 Corinthians 11.5? He clearly has no problem with such prayer or prophecy; his concern is reserved for the women doing it with uncovered heads. It seems obvious that Paul here has a particular kind of speaking in mind. I think the context here offers some clues.

First of all, he refers to the custom of "all the churches of the saints" (v. 33b). He earlier referred to such universality of custom in 1 Corinthians 11.16, where he said that women must not reject submission to their husbands. I suggest that the significance of this speaking is that it represents the women's intrusion into the role of leadership. The "others" whose task it was to weigh the prophecies were almost certainly the "teachers," the clergy mentioned in 1 Corinthians 12.28. It seems that the women of Corinth, having been taught they were spiritually equal to men in Christ, concluded from this that they were no longer in submission to their husbands and also might take a teaching role in the church. Thus when the teachers consulted together, they added their voice as well, thinking to give authoritative pronouncements along with the clergy.

This would be especially scandalous in the first century, for in that time, one was reluctant to speak in the presence of one's social superior. As Stephen Clark writes, "Most cultures, including Jewish culture of this period, observe rules of propriety of speech . . . even if (the speakers) are highly educated. For example, a disciple in first century Palestine would be very reluctant to voice an opinion in the presence of his rabbi . . . Wives would usually speak in a way that expressed their subordination to their husbands, *as would sons (including adult sons)*."[30] If even adult sons would be reluctant to speak as equals to their fathers, the spectacle of women speaking as social equals of their husbands would have provoked scandal-

---

[30]Stephen Clark, op. cit., 186–7, italics mine.

ized comment. It is this that provokes the sharp response from Paul. He insists that the woman's task is learning, and her arena is the home. The Law (already commented upon by Paul in 11.2ff) taught their subordinate role, one that precluded their giving authoritative teaching (v. 34). It is shameful for them to presume to speak in such a role in the *synaxis* (v. 35). They are to "be silent" there—not absolutely mute, but silent in the same way that the tongues-speaker and prophet is silent—i.e., silent in a particular way. The tongues-speaker is silent in that he may not speak in tongues aloud if there is no interpretation given. The prophet is silent in that he may not override the verdict of the "others" when they reject his prophecy. The women are silent in that they may not join in the public authoritative deliberations of the clergy, such as when they judge the prophecies. These verses indeed prohibit women from authoritative leadership (not just in Corinth, but "in all the churches of the saints"), but they do not prohibit other liturgical utterance.

THE TEACHING OF ST PAUL: GALATIANS 3.28

Paul's words in Galatians 3.28 are something of a favorite text with feminist Christian writers,[31] and represent for them Paul's true and abiding teaching regarding men and women. Just as Luther favored Romans 3.28, "one is justified by faith apart from works of the Law," and used this text as a prism through which to judge the rest of the New Testament (rejecting everything else which seemed to contradict it, denouncing the entire epistle of James as "an epistle of straw"), so the feminist authors favor the Galatians 3.28 text. It functions as a kind of canon within the canon, so that the texts from 1 Corinthians 11 and 14 and 1 Timothy 2 tend to be dismissed as *de facto* uncanonical, and as alien to this central and defining insight. What then is Paul's teaching in Galatians 3.28?

This text must be located within Paul's entire letter to the Galatians. The Galatians were apostasizing from the fullness of the faith, slipping back into a kind of Judaism, trusting in religion to save them rather than Christ. This was the result of listening to Paul's detractors, who slandered him,

---

[31]In her book *In Memory of Her*, Fiorenza devotes ten pages to discussing 1 Cor 11.2–16, compared to forty-three pages discussing Gal 3.28. Behr-Sigel refers to it as "the guiding line of Paul's thinking," op. cit., 153.

saying that he was not really an apostle, and that he was watering down the Gospel in order to gain their conversion. These detractors insisted that to be true disciples of the Jewish Messiah and worshippers of the Jewish God, one had to become Jewish. They had secured enough of a hearing among the Galatians that these new converts had adopted a Jewish calendar (Gal 4.10), and were now considering becoming circumcised. Paul accordingly writes to persuade them not only that circumcision is not necessary for salvation, but that reliance upon it represents apostasy from the grace of God (Gal 5.4). All they needed was faith, discipleship to Jesus. This faith, working through love (Gal 5.6), was enough to save them and make them sons of God.

The Galatians 3.28 text comes as the conclusion of a long argument, in which Paul compares the Law to the Christian faith, the revelation given in Jesus. He writes that the Law's function was as a tutor to lead us to Christ, that through faith and discipleship to Him, we might be justified (3.24). Obviously, now that we have come to Christ, the tutor is no longer necessary—our faith in Christ now gives us everything we need. Thus, they are all now "sons of God through faith in Christ Jesus" (v. 26); indeed, all of them—every single one of them—who exercised faith, who became disciples of Jesus, who were baptized into Christ, have clothed themselves with Christ (v. 27). By saying they were "clothed with Christ" (Greek=*endyō*), Paul means the baptized person has been totally covered with Christ, totally transformed. As one commentator said, "Just as a garment which one puts on quite envelops the person wearing it, and identifies his appearance and life, so the person baptized in Christ is entirely taken up in Christ."[32] So, nothing more remains for the baptized to be complete—circumcision is entirely unnecessary to our full inclusion in Christ. And this salvation is given in baptism to all without distinction: "there is neither Jew nor Greek, there is neither slave nor free, there is not male and female,[33] for you are all one in Christ Jesus" (v. 28). Paul's words

---

[32]H. Ridderbos, *Epistle of Paul to the Churches of Galatia* (Grand Rapids, MI: Eerdmans, 1953), 148.

[33]Paul does not use the phrase "neither male nor female," but rather "not male and female"—probably because the phrase "male and female" is an embedded quotation of the Genesis passage.

in Galatians 3.28 should not be lifted out of their immediate context, but must be read as flowing naturally from Galatians 3.27: it is *because* all the baptized have equally put on Christ, whatever their former state that all other distinctions have no abiding significance regarding salvation.

We see in this text that Paul first mentions the distinction between Jew and Gentile—i.e., between circumcised and uncircumcised—as being transcended, for this distinction was the main one he was combating throughout his epistle (he returns to it in his closing words in 6.15). But he goes on, because it is not simply the Jew-Gentile division that is made irrelevant in Christ. *All* social distinctions are transcended—the distinction between slave and free, and between male and female. God, through Christ and our faith in Him, is now creating a new nature, a new man (Gal 6.15, Eph 2.15), a new reality that utterly transcends all the earthly categories of this age. In this renewal, all that matters is our faith in Jesus, our becoming His obedient disciples through baptism. In this renewal there is no distinction between "Greek and Jew, circumcised and uncircumcised, barbarian, Scythian, slave and free, but Christ is all and in all" (Col 3.11). Paul chooses these categories—Jew, Gentile, barbarian, slave, free, male, female, because these were the dominant social categories of his age. Society was rigidly divided into these categories, with one disdaining the other, and with little mixing. Paul writes as a spiritual revolutionary when he declares them irrelevant to this renewal and affirms that everyone in these categories can receive a new nature through their faith in Christ. This is radically different from anything previously experienced in Judaism. Under the Old Covenant, male circumcision was the covenantal sign uniting a man with God, and women were a part of that covenant insofar as they were included in the social order ruled by Jewish men. Only free Jewish males could belong to the *qahal*, the dedicated assembly. Now, under the New Covenant, women as well as men have complete, free, and untrammeled access to God, and are full members of the New Covenant, each in their own right, without reference to anyone else. A baptized woman does not require connection with an initiated man to be initiated herself. Baptism alone provides a full and complete initiation. It is the same with the slaves: the consent of the master who owns the slave is not required by the Church before the slave can attain baptismal salvation.

A female Gentile slave and a free Jewish male are equally "sons"[34] of God and members of the redeemed community (*qahal/ekklēsia*).

We note that Paul is discussing the nature of this renewal in Christ, the "new self being renewed to a true knowledge according to the image of the One who created it" (Col 3.10). It was the nature of this renewal (and whether it needed to be supplemented with circumcision) that alone was relevant to his writing to the Galatians. That is, Paul affirms here that "there is neither Jew nor Greek, there is neither slave nor free, there is not male and female" *with respect to their salvation*. He is not commenting on the nature of slavery and the relationships of slaves to their masters, nor on the nature of gender and the relationships of husbands and wives. For that nuanced teaching regarding issues of slavery and marriage, we must look elsewhere in his teaching. But clearly Paul himself found no internal contradiction between what he wrote to the Corinthians and what he wrote to the Galatians. The distinctions between the genders (if not the rivalry and war between the genders) is the abiding obsession of our time, but it was not so with St Paul. It is exegetically questionable to isolate one verse of his teaching, draw from it conclusions alien to his thought, and then use it to oppose and refute the rest of his teaching. Moderns may see inconsistencies in Paul, but that is because they have their own feminist agendas and concerns, and in a war one looks about to find whatever weapons may be to hand. Feminist exegesis has fastened upon this one verse of Paul and pressed it into service beyond Paul's intent. While this allows one to push a feminist agenda under the Christian and Pauline banner, it does so at the cost of distorting Paul's message.

The conclusions legitimately drawn from this verse about gender are that men and women share equally in salvation, that feminine gender is no barrier to achieving the full glory of Christ, that women are not "second-class Christians." Feminist theologians assert that refusing to ordain women indeed treats women as second-class Christians, but that does not necessarily follow. "First class salvation," glory in Christ, maturity in holiness are one thing, and ordination is quite another. It remains to

---

[34]I here follow the Pauline practice of using the term "sons" rather than speak of "sons and daughters" because in the culture reflected in the New Testament it was the sons who inherited. Compare Gal 4.7: "if a son, then an heir."

be proven that there is any linkage between the two. Admittedly, if one regards the priesthood as a career, and views the entire matter through the paradigm of the civil rights movement, then denying this career on the basis of gender indeed seems discriminatory, as if those denied the career were treated as "second class." But it is just this secular paradigm that is inadequate in dealing with the realities of gender and ordination—as we hope later to show.

THE TEACHING OF ST PAUL: EPHESIANS 5

The material relevant to our study is found in Ephesians 5.21–33:

> Submit to one another out of respect [Greek=*phobos*] for Christ. [22]Wives, submit to your own husbands, as to the Lord. [23]For the husband is the head of the wife even as Christ is the head of the church, his body, and is himself its Savior. [24]Now as the church submits to Christ, so also wives should submit in everything to their husbands. [25]Husbands, love your wives, as Christ loved the church and gave himself up for her, [26]that he might sanctify her, having cleansed her by the washing of water with the word, [27]so that he might present the church to himself as glorious [Greek=*endoxos*], without spot or wrinkle or any such thing, that she might be holy and without blemish. [28]In the same way husbands should love their wives as their own bodies. He who loves his wife loves himself. [29]For no one ever hated his own flesh, but nourishes and cherishes it, just as Christ does the church, [30]because we are members of his body. [31]"Therefore a man shall leave his father and mother and hold fast to his wife, and the two shall become one flesh." [32]This is a great mystery [Greek=*mystērion*], and I am saying that it refers to Christ and the church. [33]However, let each one of you love his wife as himself, and let the wife see that she respects [Greek =*phobeō*] her husband.

A few comments may be made at the outset.

First of all, the instructions to wives and husbands are found in what scholars call a "household code" (*Haustafel*), with instructions for all in the household—wives, husbands, children, fathers, slaves, masters. What is unusual about such Christian codes is that everyone in the household is deemed worthy of instruction. In similar classic pagan instruction, only the head of the household was given instruction, for he was the one in control. Paul, on the other hand, extends that dignity to all. Also, the Christian household is characterized by the common submission to Christ. In the pagan household, the authority of the *paterfamilias* was absolute, but for Christians, only Christ's authority was absolute, and this transformed all other household relationships.

Secondly, this supreme authority of Christ meant that each one was called to serve the others, each in the ways appropriate to them. The mutual service of one for the other is what Paul refers to when he begins his instructions with the words in v. 21, "submit to one another out of respect for Christ." Strictly speaking, wives were to submit to the husbands, and not *vice-versa*; slaves were to submit to their masters, and not *vice-versa*. But Paul's basic meaning is clear: service in a Christian household is expected of all, since all respect the Lord who washed His disciples' feet. That service will take different forms; as Paul sums up in v. 33, the husband serves by loving his wife as himself, and the wife serves by respecting her husband.

The relationship of wife and husband is patterned after the relationship between the Church and Christ. This is what Paul means when he interprets the Genesis account of the creation of woman as "a great *mystērion*." A *mystērion* is a truth hidden from the world, and revealed only to the initiated—in this case, the Christians. Paul refers to this Genesis account as a great *mystērion* because its inner meaning is revealed only to those who know Christ. In the Genesis account that speaks of the man being one flesh with his wife, we see a reflection in history of the eschatological union of Christ and His body, the Church. Paul's point, to both husband and wife, is that they fulfill these typological roles. To the wives, Paul says, "You are an image of the Church, just as your husband is an image of Christ. So, as the Church submits to Christ, so you must submit to your husbands." To the husbands, Paul addresses a longer exhortation. He says, "You are an image of Christ, and your wife an image of the Church. Christ loved His bride and died for her, that she might be fulfilled and glorious. In the same way, you must love your wife and die for her, that she might

be fulfilled and joyful." Paul adds more to the husband's mandate, draw-
ing from the *mystērion* text in Genesis: the wife is "one flesh" with her
husband. "As Christ's bride is also His own body," Paul further says, "so
you husbands are one body and flesh with your wives, and you must love,
nourish and cherish them with the same solicitude that you have for your
own bodies."

In this model of leadership and submission, we see how thoroughly
the Gospel has transformed secular models of the husband's authority. A
superficial reading of these "household codes" would not detect any real
difference from the secular model, but a more careful analysis sees how
far we have come from the absolute authority of the *paterfamilias* over his
household. The radical ontological equality of man and woman is found
in their being "one flesh"—an equality Paul preserves unchanged from
the Genesis creation stories. All this would have been intolerable to the
pagan *paterfamilias*.

This transformation of the husband's authority is not surprising, for
Christ had before this transformed *all* secular authority. In Mark 10.42–
44, Christ taught the Twelve, "You know that those who are recognized
as rulers of the Gentiles lord it over them, and their great men exercise
authority over them. But it is not so among you, but whoever wishes to
become great among you shall be your servant, and whoever wishes to be
first among you shall be slave of all." Here, at a single stroke, Christ rejects
the secular understanding of authority as the power to impose one's will,
and replaces it with the power to serve. Thus, the husband's authority
translates into service for his wife, a willingness to die to self and self-will
for her sake, even "as Christ loved the church and gave Himself up for her."
We earlier said that because Adam was created before Eve, and she was
created for him, that the leadership in marriage belongs to the husband.
We now see what such leadership entails: lowliness, self-denial, loving
service, and a willingness to lay down one's life for one's beloved. Christ
provides the model for leadership—that of washing the other's feet, for
"the Son of Man came down not to be served, but to serve, and to give His
life as a ransom for many" (Mk 10.45).

It must be admitted that the Church has historically not embodied this
transformed understanding of authority as well as it might have. In par-

ticular, the bishops, priests, and other authority figures have often given the impression that authority is about power over another—thereby giving feminists the idea that women need to be ordained to redress this imbalance of power. The answer, as we will argue, is not to ordain women to the clerical office, but to transform the men in it. Pastoral authority is given solely for service and for the empowerment of others in the Church, including women, to fulfill their own lay ministries.

THE TEACHING OF ST PAUL: 1 TIMOTHY 2

The final passage we will here examine is 1 Timothy 2.8–15. It is fair to say that this text, the most explicit in prohibiting women from the pastoral office, is the least favorite text of feminist theologians. Schüssler Fiorenza seems to dismiss it entirely, and consigns it to a mere footnote in her 351-page work *In Memory of Her*, merely saying, "It must not be overlooked that 1 Timothy 2.12–15 legitimizes the prohibition of women's leadership. . . . Misogynist theology was generated because of the adaptation of the household of God to Greco-Roman patriarchal household structures."[35] Another author admits that the passage "leads many readers today to cringe and perhaps even to feel grateful that Paul himself is probably not the author."[36] Feminist author Eva Topping, sure that Paul is not the author, writes that "the genuine epistles of St Paul indicate that indeed women . . . held positions of leadership." She accounts for the passage, which she dates in "the end of the second century," as "a reaction against women's freedom."[37] But whether or not Paul is the author of the text,[38] it remains in the New Testament, which is authoritative for Christians, and therefore it must be squarely faced.[39]

[35]Schüssler Fiorenza, op. cit., 336.

[36]Bouteneff, op. cit., 52.

[37]Topping, op. cit., 44, 104.

[38]For a scholarly defence of Pauline authorship, see Donald Guthrie's *New Testament Introduction* (London: Inter-Varsity Press, 1975).

[39]Some have sought to minimize the importance of this text by suggesting that the author's counsel was limited to the women of Ephesus, the city to which his epistle was addressed. There is nothing in the text to remotely suggest such a limitation, and the reasons given for the limitation are rooted in the created order, not the local circumstances. Rather, the limitations set in 1Tim 2 find echo in 1 Cor 14. In 1 Cor 14.33–34, Paul explicitly says that his ruling and practice is found "in all the churches of the saints."

The passage in question reads as follows.

[8]I desire then that in every place the men should pray, lifting holy hands without anger or quarreling; [9]likewise also that women should adorn themselves in respectable apparel, with modesty and self-control, not with braided hair and gold or pearls or costly attire, [10]but with what is proper for women who profess godliness—with good works. [11]Let a woman learn quietly with all submissiveness. [12]I do not permit a woman to teach or to exercise authority over a man; rather, she is to remain quiet. [13]For Adam was formed first, then Eve; [14]and Adam was not deceived, but the woman was quite deceived and became a transgressor. [15]Yet she will be saved through childbearing—if they continue in faith and love and holiness, with self-control.

The text does not deal at great length with the relationship between men and women or offer a theological framework for it (as in 1 Cor 11.3ff), but focuses on the practical matters of "how one ought to conduct oneself in the household of God" (1 Tim 3.15). After dealing with the primary necessity of the church's making "entreaties, prayers, petitions and thanksgivings on behalf of all" (1 Tim 2.1), the text goes on to deal briefly with an exhortation directed to men, and then to women. Its main concern for the men is that they should pray "without anger or quarreling" (v. 8)—obviously because such anger was a problem. The men's lead in prayer is assumed, not because the women were forbidden to pray (compare Paul's assumption that women would both pray and prophesy in 1 Cor 11.5), but because men offered most of the prayers—a reference, I submit, to the prayers offered by the men as local *episcopoi* (compare 3.1ff).

The author then goes on to address the women, saying that they "similarly" (Greek *hōsautōs*) should strive for internal holiness. A practical problem of feminine luxuriousness is addressed and censured in v. 9–10. And then comes the further censure of v. 11–14. The woman's role was to "learn quietly with all submissiveness." She was not to "teach or exercise authority over a man." It seems that the women of Ephesus to whom the author wrote had the same temptations as the women of Corinth—to conclude that their new status and freedom in Christ meant they also could assume the role of authoritative "teachers and shepherds" (Paul's term for the *episcopoi* or clergy in Eph 4.11).

The author denies this is a valid conclusion, and, as in 1 Corinthians 14.34–35, he exhorts them to maintain a role of subordination to their husbands. Their authority is not located in the Christian *synaxis*. There women are forbidden "to teach" (Greek=*didaskō*)—i.e., to exercise the ministry of a *didaskalos* (so-called in Acts 13.1, Eph 4.11, Jas 3.1). This teaching role was a part of the ministry of an *episcopos* or *presbyteros* (1 Tim 3.1, 5.17), the terms being used here interchangeably (Titus 1.5, 7). This teaching ministry included "exercising authority" (v. 12, Greek =*authenteō*) or "ruling" (Greek=*proistēmi*), and as such was incompatible with the woman's subordinate role. In other words, the pastoral office of bishop/presbyter is denied her. Regarding authoritative teaching, "she is to remain quiet" (Greek=*hēsychia*). (In Paul's other instructions, we have seen that this was not a total silence, since she could both pray and prophesy. Rather, the ban here is specifically on authoritative teaching in the *synaxis*.)

The reason for this prohibition is not found in the culture of the day. It was not that women were then disqualified because of their (supposed) lack of education. Indeed, many women were well educated and exercised important roles in society. Roman society knew of women goldsmiths, physicians, land-estate owners, and bosses in shipyards.[40] Many Christian women in the early Church were theologically educated, such as St Melania of Constantinople, the deaconess Olympias, and St Gregory of Nyssa's sister Macrina, to whom he refers as his "Teacher." A circle of educated women gathered around Theodosia, the sister of the bishop of Iconium. St Jerome dedicated many of his commentaries to educated women. Indeed, Jerome (often criticized for his supposed misogyny) recommended that a girl read the works of Cyprian, Athanasius and Hilary.[41] These women had no lack of education, and Roman society saw nothing wrong with educating women. Thus, Paul's rationale for prohibiting the pastoral office to women should not be sought in women's supposed ignorance or educational deficit.

---

[40]Hauke, *Women in the Priesthood?* (San Francisco: Ignatius Press, 1988), 341.
[41]Ibid., 433–434.

Rather, the rationale is found in the creation stories (even as Paul grounded his instructions regarding women speaking in the *synaxis* in the creation stories in 1 Cor 11 and 1 Cor 14). The author assumes knowledge of the story, and merely says, "Adam was created first, then Eve." A hostile approach to this text will easily dismiss the rationale as simplistic and invalid (one author speaks of it as having "all the moral force of a playground claim to the jungle gym"[42]), but this is to show insensitivity to Paul's close reading of the Genesis narrative. As we saw in our examination of 1 Corinthians 11, the thought here is of the wife being created *for* the husband and as a helper for *him*. This certainly runs contrary to the canons of our politically correct egalitarian culture, but it is not irrational or inconsistent with the creation stories of Genesis. Bluntly put, if the argument here has little emotional resonance or moral force for us, it is only because it contradicts our own cherished presuppositions and biases. The author presupposes the authority for Christians of the Genesis stories,[43] and concludes that when Eve stepped out of her subordinate role to lead her husband, she inevitably "was quite deceived" (Greek=*exapataō*, a stronger verb than "deceived," *apataō,* used earlier in the sentence). His conclusion is clear: by rejecting their original role and becoming their husbands' leader, the women of Paul's day run the risk of being deceived, as Eve was. The insistence on assuming the authoritative pastoral office would lead the women into becoming "transgressors."

Women's authority, therefore, was not located in the Christian *synaxis*, but in the home. There they rule their households. This authority should not be minimized. The (masculine) ruler of the house is called the *oikodespotēs* in Matthew 24.43 (translated "the head of the house" in the NASB). The cognate verb (*oikodespoteō*) is used of women in 1 Timothy 5.14, where the woman is counseled to rule the house (translated rather weakly as "keep house" in the NASB, with unfortunate associations; the RSV translates it as "rule their households"—surely more in keeping with what the author envisioned). This feminine role involved "childbearing." It does not mean, as some commentators have perversely suggested, that Paul says that women are saved by bearing children, rather than through

---

[42]Bouteneff, op. cit., 52.

[43]Dismissed by Topping as a "primitive folk-tale," op. cit., 50.

faith in Christ. Nor is the idea (advanced by some) that women will be saved "through the bearing of the Child"—i.e., through Christ. That is true, but since it applies to men as well as women, it is hardly the point. Nor is the intended sense that women will be saved/preserved as they bear children—i.e., will suffer no death in childbirth, but will be brought safely through.[44] These suggestions make rather heavier weather of the text than necessary. The intended sense is surely that women will find their salvation in the domestic realm, rather than in the Christian *synaxis*. Why specify childbearing as characteristic of that realm? As Behr-Sigel says, Paul "is obviously not trying to make biological maternity women's sole vocation, but rather to honor her in the function that is hers alone: bringing children into the world. The point is directed against certain heretical gnostics who disparaged sex, marriage and procreation.[45] In contrast, Paul associates maternity with the life of faith for the Christian woman."[46] Paul goes on to add a small clarifying footnote—this saving childbearing presupposes the life of faith, love, holiness, and self-control. That is, women need the same life of faith as do men (compare the requirements of the men in Titus 2.2).

The Teaching of St Peter: 1 Peter 3

Finally we look at a text in 1 Peter 3.1–7. Once again, the Petrine authorship of the text is irrelevant to our examination of its teaching.

> [1]Likewise, wives, submit to your own husbands, so that even if some do not obey the Word, they may be won without a word by the conduct of their wives, [2]when they see your respectful and pure conduct. [3]Do not let your adorning be external—the braiding of hair and the putting on of gold jewelery, or the clothing you wear—[4]but let your adorning be the hidden person of the heart with the imperishable beauty of a gentle and quiet spirit, which in God's sight is very precious. [5]For this is how the holy women who hoped in God used to adorn themselves,

[44]Which seems to be the intended sense of the NASB, which translates *sōzō* 'saved' as "preserved."

[45]Compare the denunciation of such heresies in 1 Tim 4.1–3.

[46]Behr-Sigel, op. cit., 72.

by submitting to their own husbands, [6]as Sarah obeyed Abraham, calling him lord. And you are her children, if you do good and do not fear anything that is frightening. [7]Likewise, husbands, live with your wives according to knowledge, showing honor to the woman as the weaker vessel, since they are co-heirs with you of the grace of life, so that your prayers may not be hindered.

This epistle, written to churches that had many newly baptized members (compare the reference to the new birth and to being new born babes in 1.23 and 2.2), was also written to a church under stress. The author refers to the proof of their faith being "tested by fire" (1.7); he urges them, "do not fear their intimidation and do not be troubled" (3.14). He speaks of the "fiery ordeal which comes upon you for your testing" (4.12), of "your adversary the devil" who "prowls about like a roaring lion, seeking someone to devour" (5.8), and urges them to resist the temptation to apostasize, "knowing that the same experiences of suffering are being accomplished by your brethren" (5.9). Against this background of a hostile, watching world, the author's basic concern is that all must "keep (their) behavior excellent among the Gentiles," and thus "submit for the Lord's sake to every human creation"—i.e., to all the proper institutions, including the "the king" and "governors sent by him" (2.13–14). This decision to live in such a way as to commend the gospel to the world worked itself out in various ways: servants were to be submissive to their masters (2.18), wives were to be submissive to their husbands (3.1f), and husbands were likewise to live with their wives according to knowledge, granting them honor (3.7). This necessity for the Christians to demonstrate their "respectability" does not determine the nature of the counsel given. The Christians would "honor all men, love the brotherhood, fear God, and honor the king" (2.17), regardless of the political climate. But the hostile political climate does throw these perennial obligations into high relief.

Furthermore, in his advice to slaves, wives, and husbands, Peter is not writing a treatise on slavery or marriage, nor is he saying everything that could be said about slavery or marriage. Rather, he is applying to specific situations his general exhortation that *all* Christians are to "submit themselves for the Lord's sake to every human institution" in the several relationships in which they find themselves (2.13). It would be a mistake therefore to conclude from this that the wife's only or main responsibility is submission. Rather, in talking about how all Christians should be in submission, he specifies how this general submission works itself out in the lives of Christian married women. Other components in the relationship between husband and wife, such as her authority in the home, and her authority over the body of her husband (cf. 1 Cor 7.4) he leaves unaddressed in this passage. Having looked at this background, we may now examine the passage in more detail.

The wives are "likewise" to submit to their husbands, the "likewise" (Greek=*homoiōs*) referring back to the necessity of slaves submitting to their masters (2.18)—though, as the text makes clear, the quality of each submission is different. Realizing that the Christians live in the midst of an unbelieving world, the author acknowledges a possible worst-case scenario, and says that even if the husbands "do not obey the Word" (i.e., are not Christians), they may thus be won over by the behavior of their wives. (A possible worst-case scenario is envisioned in 2.18 also, when it is admitted that some masters may be "perverse" and unreasonable: such cases do not absolve the Christian slaves of their responsibility, nor justify rebellion.) Peter urges the wives to have as their main focus internal beauty, not external (compare similar counsel in 1 Tim 2.9–10). True and lasting beauty is that of "a gentle and quiet spirit" (v. 4), which acknowledges the husband's leadership and does not rebel against it. The example of Sarah is proffered as encouragement, for she "obeyed Abraham, calling him 'lord'" (v. 6)—the usual term for husband in her culture, and a reference to Genesis 18.12.[47] The main accent is on the necessity of wives to submit to their husbands, even the pagan ones.

This advice to wives (which begins with the word "likewise," connecting it with the previous advice to slaves and to Christians in general; see 2.13, 18) must not be separated from the advice to the husbands—which also begins with "likewise," so that the necessity of submission and service is common to all Christians, be they slaves, wives, or husbands. This may be

---

[47]That there was more to the relationship between Abraham and Sarah than wifely submission can be seen from their interaction in Gen 16.1–6, where Sarah's vehement demands regarding Hagar meet with a meek and compliant response from Abraham.

stressed: the husbands "likewise" are to show the same measure of service and love to their wives as their wives do to them. (We are reminded of the advice to wives and husbands in Ephesians 5.21ff, which also begins with the general exhortation for all to "submit to one another." In this sense, service is not a one-way street, with wives doing all the serving. Husbands have their own call to serve their wives also.) If the wives are advised to serve by submitting to their husbands' leadership, the husbands are to serve by "living with (their) wives according to knowledge" (Greek =*kata gnōsin*). What does this mean? The RSV translates it "considerately"; the NASB "in an understanding way"; other translations assume this *gnosis* is knowledge of the wife's weakness (compare J.B. Phillips' *New Testament in Modern English*: "try to understand the wives you live with"). I suggest, however, that the knowledge here refers to knowledge of God (compare Paul's use of the word in 1 Cor 8.1f, Col 2.3), so that the author is telling the husbands to live with their wives knowing what God demands, living with them as Christians, living differently than pagan husbands would. (This knowledge thus contrasts with their former "ignorance," when they lived as pagans; compare 1 Peter 1.14. The contrast between their former pagan and present Christian states pervades the letter; see also 1.18, 22; 2.10, 25; 4.3–4.) However *kata gnōsin* is to be translated, the result of such *gnosis* is that the husband shows honor to the wife. She is described here as "the weaker vessel"—a reference to her vulnerability. Consequently, his responsibility is to protect her and care for her.

This care must be given since the wife is a "co-heir" (Greek= *sygklēronomos*) with him of the grace of life. That is, husband and wife together are called to inherit eternal life. The unity of the two is stressed— the wife is not simply another "heir," but a "co-heir"; it is stated that she inherits life "with (him)." In short, their spiritual life is bound up inextricably together. That is why, if the husband does not show her "honor," his "prayers" will be "hindered." God will judge him for not showing her honor and caring for her, and will reject his prayers. We note that this constitutes a veiled threat to the husbands, and thus that the exhortation to the husbands is every bit as emphatic as that to the wives.

Summary of the Teaching of Scripture

In the Genesis texts, we saw both equality and subordination in the presentation of male and female. In the first creation story, both man and woman jointly shared the divine image and divine authority to rule the earth—both were *adam*. (The word *adam* functioned to describe both the human species, and also the first male of that species.) In this joint sharing, there is absolute unity and equality. We saw in the second story of the creation and fall, this primordial unity also involves the subordination of the woman to the man—i.e., of the wife to the husband—but that this subordination is the free subordination of ontological equals, for she is different from the animals, being "bone of his bones and flesh of his flesh." This equality, even in the subordination of one to the other, is witnessed in their becoming "one flesh." The Fall was not the source of this subordination, since the subordination preceded it. The Fall simply meant that each of them would fulfill their divine destinies in pain and weakness, since they had lost access to the tree of life. Even after their fall, the dignity of each remained. And if the subordination of the woman is seen in her being named by Adam, her dignity is seen in what he names her: "Life."

The Genesis texts remain fundamental for later Christian understanding of gender, beginning with the teaching of Christ Himself. Though He opposed much of the scribal interpretations and distortions of the Law, He referred His disciples back to the original intent of the Law as the means of correcting these distortions. Thus the scribal allowance of divorce (based on their reading of Deut 24) was answered by Christ by His referring back to the Genesis accounts as containing God's true and final will. He did not set aside the Genesis accounts as belonging to the "old Law," but regarded them as authoritative and paradigmatic for His disciples. Further, the complementary themes in Genesis of equality and subordination find an echo in Christ's dealing with women: He accepted as disciples all who approached in humility regardless of gender (showing that He recognized the equality of women), but did not choose women for inclusion in the authority-laden Twelve (showing that He recognized their subordination).

In the works of St Paul, we saw him following in the steps of His Master. That is, just as Christ accepted women as co-equal disciples with men, so Paul also sees women as co-equal disciples of Christ, sharing a salvation and glory equal to them. Paul famously declares there to be "no male and female" in Christ (Gal 3.28), and allows women to pray and prophesy in the Christian assembly (1 Cor 11.5). He says that "in the Lord," the woman is not independent of the man and the man is not independent of the woman, but rather that both are mutually interdependent (1 Cor 11.11). The husband and wife therefore are to "submit to one another," by serving each other in ways appropriate to each (Eph 5.21), since they are "one flesh" (Eph 5.31).

As Christ not only affirmed the equality of man and woman, but also the subordination of wife to husband, so also Paul affirmed this subordination. Paul declared the wife had her husband as her head/leader (1 Cor 11.2), and insisted that public deportment in the *synaxis* reflect this. He declared the wife to be the glory of the husband (1 Cor 11.7). Furthermore, he denied the women a role in the authoritative judging of prophecies in the *synaxis*, and insisted they keep silent from those deliberations and decisions, saying that this subordination was mandated by the Law, the original Genesis stories (1 Cor 14.34). Paul forbade women a teaching or governing role in the *synaxis*, such as was exercised by the *episcopos* or *presbyteros* (1 Tim 2.12), and he grounded this prohibition in the Genesis stories.

All in all, we see a remarkable consistency in these texts. All these texts reveal a vision of women as both equal to men and as subordinate, and see this as anchored in the original Genesis narratives. Of course if Paul indeed wrote all these texts himself, such consistency is not at all surprising. We see too that there is no break or change between the teaching of Christ and His apostle, St Paul. It is not the case that Christ promoted one vision of gender, and St Paul later distorted and altered it. Rather, Paul continues the teaching of his Lord.

Further, we see there is no break or change between the teaching of Paul in (for example) Galatians 3.28 and in Ephesians 5. It is not the case that the "authentic Paul" promoted a vision of liberation and equality, and a later teacher, unhappy with the apostolic deposit, altered and countered it, promoting a contrary vision of subordination and oppression. Rather, both themes of equality and subordination are found throughout Paul's writings. Obviously, since these writings are occasional and not systematic treatises on gender, Paul does not say everything that could be said every time he puts pen to paper. Which part of his multi-faceted understanding of men-women relationships he speaks of depends upon the occasion. To the Galatians, he speaks of their equality. To Timothy, he speaks of their subordination. To the Corinthians and the Ephesians, he speaks of both. In this regard Paul's first letter to the Corinthians is especially important. Feminist critics are fond of contrasting the early Pauline Galatians 3.28 with the later ostensibly non-Pauline 1 Timothy 2.12 and asserting that the writer of Galatians could not have written 1 Timothy. But the subordinationist teaching of 1 Timothy 2.12 is equally found in 1 Corinthians 11.2ff, proving that Paul could easily be the author of both. What modern feminism views as irreconcilable dichotomies were simply complementary parts of Paul's multi-faceted teaching. In short, feminist agendas push modern Christians to see as contradiction what the ancient Christians saw as complexity.

In the first Epistle of St Peter, we saw the same twin themes of equality and subordination. That is, he taught that women were equal to men, in that they were "co-heirs of the grace of life," so that for the husband to refuse to grant his wife honor would impede his own spiritual life. But Peter also taught that women were to be subordinate to their husbands, as imitators of Sarah. Though not referring to the original creation stories, Peter does anchor his teaching in Genesis, seeing this subordination as part of the lasting legacy of the Law for Christians. The fact that Peter's teaching mirrors Paul's is further confirmation that these twin themes of equality and subordination were not simply their own personal views, but were expressions of their Lord's approach. This is all the more likely since we see these themes manifested in Christ's ministry and teaching, and also in the Genesis stories, which He set forth as authoritative for His disciples.

It remains to ask how these teachings might be applied today, since it is obvious that they are culturally expressed in terms of the first century. For example, first-century Corinth considered short hair on women as scandalous (1 Cor 11.6), and head-coverings were a sign of domestic respectability. It is culturally otherwise now, so that no one seeing a woman with uncovered head in our churches concludes that the woman is somehow repudiating her husband's leadership. What is the abiding significance of this teaching? I suggest that though the teaching is *culturally expressed* (everything is culturally expressed, in every age), it is not thereby *culturally conditioned*. That is, it is not the case that the authors of this teaching only spoke as men of their times, and with no other wisdom but that available to other men of their day. As we have seen, the teaching of Paul and Peter found its ultimate source in the teaching of Christ, and this had some significant divergences from the culture of their day.

In applying their teaching in other cultures such as our own, we need therefore to look for the underlying principles. The Church teaches that women are equal to men, and that the wife is subordinate to her husband's leadership. How this subordination is expressed will differ from place to place and from century to century. In the first century, the subordination was expressed in women's use of head-coverings during the *synaxis*, and in their not taking part in public deliberations, such as when the others (i.e., the clergy, as we would say today) judged the prophecies. In our own time, head-coverings do not have this cultural significance, and public debate is almost never limited, even in the presence of one's social superiors. But the underlying principle still remains, and women should still dress and comport themselves in ways consistent with their commitment to their husbands. Also, the pastoral office remains closed to women, since the pastoral office involves exercising authority over men in the church (including the husband), and this is inconsistent with women's subordination.

CHAPTER 3

The Witness of the Fathers

Approaching the Fathers

*I*n much Christian feminist reading of history, a golden age of egalitarianism in the early church was followed by its overthrow, as the Church Fathers forsook the egalitarian vision of Jesus and of the "authentic Paul" and replaced it with the usual patriarchal views of the secular society around them. As Topping sums up, "By the end of the second century, the situation had changed. The days of the egalitarian church had ended . . . the church adopted a policy of cultural accommodation to prevailing patriarchal societal patterns."[1] Many feminist theologians date 1 Timothy, Ephesians, and a 1 Corinthians 14.34–35 interpolation to this period as well, leaving as the authentic New Testament only the bits deemed acceptable to modern feminism. (It's a tried strategy; ask Marcion.) The Church Fathers, therefore, are the villains of the piece, and words like "misogynist" are often used to describe them.

Admittedly, some writers in the Church provide plenty of ammunition for moderns ready to take aim at them. Think of Tertullian (who admittedly seemed to have what we would today call "issues" about practically everything): "*You* (women) are the devil's gateway, *you* are the unsealer of that tree, *you* are the first forsaker of the divine law, *you* so lightly crushed the image of God, the man Adam. Because of *your* punishment, that is, death, even the Son of God had to die." (*On the Dress of Women* 1.1.2) Granted that he is speaking rhetorically, by anyone's figuring the critique is one-sided and over the top. And other passages could be culled from other writers. What then are we to say about the Church Fathers?

---

[1]Topping, op. cit., 104.

The first thing to say is what Behr-Sigel said, namely that "Patristic anthropology is not a monolithic block."[2] To speak of "the views of the Fathers" is a bit like speaking of "the views of Western civilization" or "the views of Americans," in that these include many various and even contradictory voices. This is hardly surprising, since the Christian writing we are considering includes voices spanning centuries and continents. Western views are often different from eastern views (for example, in their approach to sex within marriage), and different regions had different emphases. The extant writings of the Fathers, collected by Migne, are exceedingly large.[3] Accordingly, we cannot expect anything like uniformity, much less an identical detailed exegesis of the Scriptural passages.

What we *can* expect, and what we find, is a group of men genuinely striving to be true to their Scriptural inheritance. Obviously they worked within their own ages and cultures, inheriting certain views of women and their roles from those cultures. Some were able to discern how the Scriptural views about women differed from the secular views of their time, and some were less able. They inherited, after all, a complex and multi-faceted view of men and women, and it is not surprising if some focused mostly on the parts of Scripture that reinforced the views current in secular society. (It is a timeless temptation, and modern feminist Christians are not immune to it.) But all in all, if we look at the patristic writings and their *phronēma* or mindset as a whole, we find the same themes expounded in the Scriptures. Some Fathers may not have stressed certain of those themes enough for our modern taste, but, to be fair, they were addressing problems of their own day, not ours. It is unrealistic and unfair to demand that they speak to our issues—or even to give what we might regard as a balanced view every time they wrote. (In this last regard, it must be remembered also that much of what survives is their preaching and Bible study. That is, they were writing to meet this or that need, to respond to this or that occasion, not writing a systematic theology.)

Our modern obsessions are foreign to all the ancients, including ancient women. We will be disappointed if we insist that the Fathers share

[2]Op. cit., 83.
[3]Migne's *Patrologia Graeca* runs to 161 volumes; the *Patrologia Latina* runs to 217 volumes.

our indignation at what we regard as discrimination and strive to correct it, when none of the ancients, including women, regarded it in this light. Just as St Paul regarded subordination as essentially compatible with equality, so did the Fathers and people of their day generally. The question is not, "Were the Fathers egalitarian like us?" We know they were not. The question is, "Did the Fathers deal fairly with the Scriptural teaching they inherited?"

We look at the Fathers, therefore, to find a broad and generalized consensus about gender. Our task is to see if the teaching of Scripture, examined in the previous chapter, survives in their work, or (conversely) if they dropped one part of the total Scriptural "package" and promoted only those parts which conformed to the secular society of their day. In other words, our task is to see whether the twin themes of women's equality with men and the wife's subordination to the husband survive in their work as a whole. I submit that these themes did survive, and that therefore theirs was not simply an abandonment of the biblical teaching in favor of the patriarchalism of their day. Rather, theirs was a patriarchalism, but it was a patriarchalism informed and modified by the New Testament. (The degree to which the church of their day to which they preached heeded their call and heard these biblical modifications is, of course, another story. But the fault for this cannot be laid entirely at the feet of the preachers.)

The Theme of Equality between Men and Women

As said above, the patristic literature is a vast ocean; we can do no more than dip our toe into it, assembling a few witnesses to the biblical teaching which the Fathers inherited.

Perhaps not unexpectedly, St John Chrysostom has lots to say. The Golden-Mouth is the preacher *par excellence*, and his practical goal was the sanctification of his hearers. He strived to exegete the Scriptures in such a way as to inspire his audience to holiness, not to produce a treatise about gender. Because of this, his views on the equality of men and women must be gleaned in passing.

St John refers to Galatians 3.28, expanding it with a preacher's freedom. He says, "Whether slave or free, whether Greeks or barbarians or

Scythians, unlearned or learned, female or male . . . all are deemed worthy of the same privilege. For faith and the grace of the Spirit, removing the inequality caused by worldly things, has molded them all into one form, stamped them with one impress of the King" (*Homily on St John*, 10). With these words, Chrysostom acknowledges that both genders "are deemed worthy of the same privilege" of being "stamped with one and same impress of the King." As far as salvation is concerned, "faith and the grace of the Spirit remove the inequalities" of these "worldly" categories. In the realm of the King's salvation, there is complete equality between male and female. What matters ultimately to Chrysostom is not "worldly things," but growth in virtue for the Lord's sake. And for him it is self-evident that both genders have a level playing field. Women are not evil by nature or more prone to vice than men. As he elsewhere says, "You see everywhere vice and virtue not differentiated by nature [i.e., by gender], but by character" (*Homily 4 on Hosea*).

Furthermore, Chrysostom is clear that men and women were created equal, and he stresses this to secure the woman's proper honor from her husband. In discussing the creation story, he says, "Before [the first] sin, the woman was like the man. Indeed, when God molded the woman, He used the words in creating her that He had used when He fashioned man. In addition, He said, 'Let us make for him a helper.' And He does not call her simply 'a helper,' but 'a helper like him,' once more showing the equality of honor" (*Discourse 4 on Genesis*). He stresses this equal balance of honor in his comments on 1 Corinthians 11.11: "Having talked about the glory of the man, Paul now re-establishes the balance so as not to exalt the man beyond what is his due, nor to depress the woman . . . each one of the two is the cause of the other, God being the cause of all" (*Homilies on Corinthians* 26.5). Clearly, the ontological equality of the genders is not lost upon the preacher of Antioch and Constantinople.

We may next look at the Cappodocian Fathers, beginning with St Basil the Great. He also grasps the equal honor bestowed upon woman at the creation. In his tenth homily on Psalm 1, he writes, "Why does the prophet David [in writing "Blessed is the man" at the beginning of the psalm] single out only man and proclaim him blessed? Does he thereby exclude women from blessedness? By no means. For the virtue of man and woman is the same, since creation is equally honored in both; therefore there is the same reward for both. . . . They whose nature is alike have the same reward. Why then when Scripture made mention of man did it leave women unnoticed? Because it believed that it was sufficient to indicate the whole through the more authoritative part." Here St Basil writes like the pastor he is. Though the Greek *anēr* (translating the Hebrew *ish*) in Psalm 1.1 usually means "man" as opposed to "woman," Basil is concerned to be inclusive, and to stress that the blessedness available does not "exclude women." He knows that "creation is equally honored" in both genders, in that both genders equally share the image of God. Like Chrysostom, Basil sees an equality of opportunity for both men and woman, since "they whose nature is alike have the same reward" when they attain virtue.

This pastoral concern to ascribe to women their proper honor is found also in Basil's words on the creation of men and women. The Greek text of Genesis read, "And God made the man [=*anthrōpon*] according to His image." The word *anthrōpos* means "man" in the sense of "human being," but Basil is not content until he clarifies that this includes the woman as well as the man. In his *Homily on the Origin of Man* (1.18), he says, "So that no one through ignorance takes the word 'man' [in the Genesis text] to mean only the masculine sex, the Scriptures add 'man and woman He created them.' The wife also like the husband, has the privilege of being created in the image of God. Their two natures are equally honorable; equal are their virtues; equal are their rewards; and alike are their condemnations. Let no woman say, 'I am weak.' Strength is in the soul. Since assuredly the image of God works the same honor [wherever it is found], let the virtue and good works of both the husband and the wife be equally honorable. . . . The virtuous women possess what belongs to the image. Woman, you have obtained the likeness of God by goodness, patience, attentive listening, by loving others and your brothers." This passage is particularly remarkable for its time, for women were proverbially considered weak. Against this background, whatever outer weakness women may possess, Basil insists that "no woman" should say "I am weak," since true weakness or strength is found "in the soul," and there, in the inner souls, women have the same strength as men, since they equally share the same image of God as men do. What matters is not gender, but virtue.

This recognition of inner equality is shared by Basil's friend, St Gregory the Theologian: "The same creator for man and woman, for both of them the same clay, the same image, the same law, the same death and the same resurrection" (Discourse 37.6). By the rhetorical repetition of the words "the same," Gregory stresses the ontological equality of both genders— both share the same origin from humble clay, both share the same divine image, both are beholden to the same divine law, both share the same death for transgressing that law, and both will share the same resurrection and glory. Here, in the entire sweep of redemption, man has no pre-eminence over woman, but both stand side by side as equals before God.

With Basil's brother St Gregory of Nyssa, we find ourselves rubbing shoulders somewhat with their mentor Origen. For Gregory, saying that the soul is made in the image of God means that it has a likeness to God and that therefore things foreign to the divine nature must be essentially foreign to it also. Thus he writes in his *On the Soul and the Resurrection*, "[The Scripture's teaching that] the soul is a likeness of God has proclaimed that everything which is alien to God is outside the definition of the soul."[4] This provides a bit of a dilemma for him, since gender is foreign to God, and yet humanity is gendered. He solves the dilemma by positing two creations—that of the essential soul and that of differentiation into gender.

In his *On the Making of Man* (16) he again says, "[The Scripture] says, 'God created man; in the image of God He created him.' That is an end of the creation of that which was made 'in the image': then it resumes the account of creation and says, 'male and female He created them.' I presume that everyone knows that this is a departure from the [divine] Prototype, for 'in Christ Jesus,' as the apostle says, 'there is neither male nor female,' Yet the phrase 'male and female He created them' declares that man is thus divided." In this passage, Gregory is asserting that man is indeed made in the image of God in the inner soul, which is common to both genders, and that gender differentiation is somehow less basic to humanity than this inner soul. For him, the divine Prototype (witnessed to by Gal 3.28) is genderless. Therefore, the divine image in humanity is genderless too. Put differently, the soul is neither male nor female. Gregory's thought, as

---

[4]St Gregory of Nyssa, *On the Soul and the Resurrection*, translated by Catherine P. Roth, Popular Patristics Series 12 (Crestwood, NY: St Vladimir's Seminary Press, 1993), 51.

he tries to shoe-horn Origen into a more Orthodox framework, is very complicated. In Gregory's positing a double creation, Bouteneff says that Gregory is not so much thinking of two created realms, as "two stages, or better, two aspects of the same creation," the first aspect being "purely conceptual, as distinct from its being realized in substance."[5]

Heavy stuff, this. But for our purposes it is important to see that Gregory sees the same divine image in both men and women. At the end of the day, he stands alongside his brother Basil, his friend Gregory—and his sister Macrina, whom he called his "teacher" (immortalized in his work *On the Soul and the Resurrection*[6]).

We may yet examine a few more voices before leaving the east. Clement of Alexandria, in his *Miscellanies* (4.8) wrote: "As there is sameness [between men and women] with respect to the soul, she will attain to the same virtue, but as there is difference with respect to the particular construction of the body, she is destined for childbearing and house-keeping . . . women are to philosophize equally with men." Clement, who styled himself a gnostic (though not of the same ilk as the gnostic heretics) had a warm appreciation for philosophy, the "love of wisdom." He acknowledged what we have called the twin themes of woman's equality and submission. Women possessed "sameness" with men "with respect to the soul," so that they could "attain to the same virtue" as men. They were therefore the equals of men in their souls. It was "with respect to the particular construction of the body" (notice the philosophical delicacy!) that they were different, since sexual activity for them meant they were "destined for childbearing and housekeeping." Despite this domestic subordination, women could still "philosophize equally with men." The significance of this last should not be minimized, given Clement's great esteem for philosophy. For him, philosophy was the path to salvation and glory, so that Clement is saying that woman's domestic role is no barrier to a sanctification and glory equal to man's.

This teaching of ontological equality (or equality of soul, to use the ancient term) is found also in St Cyril of Jerusalem. The great pastor of

---

[5]Bouteneff, op. cit., 157.

[6]*On the Soul and the Resurrection*, p. 51: "As our sister and teacher still remained in this life . . ."—and he refers to her thus in many places throughout the treatise.

the Holy City writes: "The soul is immortal, and all souls are alike, both
of men and women, for only the members of the body are distinguished"
(*Catechetical Lectures* 4.20). His teaching is therefore identical to Clement's: "All souls are alike," regardless of gender. It is only "the members of
the body" that are "distinguished," and where domestic differences may
be found.

Before leaving this theme of equality, we may include a western patristic voice, that of St Ambrose of Milan. In his work *On Paradise* (10.48)
Ambrose writes: "It is not beside the point to note that the woman was
not made from the same earth from which Adam was formed, but from
Adam's own rib. From this point we learn that the bodily nature of man
and woman is one, one the source of the human race . . . since God wished
to constitute one human nature, He took away the possibility of multiple
and diverse natures of his created being by beginning from one source."
In referring to them sharing the same "bodily nature" and precluding the
"possibility of multiple and diverse natures," Ambrose asserts the essential
unity and equality of men and women.

The Theme of Subordination of Wife to Husband

We begin once more with St John Chrysostom. While accepting that both
men and women are equally "stamped with the impress of the King" (see
above), he also recognizes the subordination of wife to husband. When
Chrysostom reads in 1 Corinthians 11.7 that the man is "the image and
glory of God, but the woman is the glory of man," he concludes that the
image of God as well as the glory of God is unique to the man, and that
woman does not share in God's image. But by "image," Chrysostom did
not mean what (for example) St Basil meant. But, as Chrysostom says,
"[The word] 'image' [in Gen 1.26] is not meant in regard to essence, but
in regard to authority. . . . To grasp the point that the form of man is not
that of God, listen to what Paul says: 'For the man ought not to be veiled,
for he is the image of and glory of God. But woman is the glory of man'
. . . Not so, according to our opponents, who argue that not only the man
must have the 'image' but the woman as well. Our answer is that the man
and the woman do have one form, one distinctive character, one likeness,

Then why is the man said to be in the 'image of God' and the woman not? Because what Paul says about the 'image' does not pertain to form. The 'image' has rather to do with authority, and this only the man has" (Discourse 2 on Genesis). So, for St John, the wife has less authority than her husband, though they share the same ontological equality—in his words, the same "form, character, likeness, essence."

Consistent with this (following the Pauline teaching), Chrysostom says that women may not be ordained to positions of clerical authority, such as the episcopate and presbyterate. He acknowledges woman's virtue, and says that even such ascetic exploits as "fasting, sleeping on the bare ground, and prolonged vigils, acting as champion to the wronged . . . could readily be performed by . . . women as well. If however it is a matter of being entrusted with direction of a church and with the care of so many souls, then not only must the entire female sex step back from so great a task, but also the majority of males" (*On the Priesthood*, 2.2). The issue for St John is not one therefore of insufficient holiness. Women can be just as holy as men. The issue is one of authority and subordination, so that as regards "being entrusted with the direction of a church" (which requires exercising authority over men), "the entire female sex must step back."

The witness of St John's contemporary, Theodore of Mopsuestia, agrees: "While Paul forbids women teaching in church," (he writes in his *Commentary on 1 Timothy,* at 1 Tim 2.11), "he very much wants them to exercise their authority in the home as the teachers of virtue."[7] Once again we see the same strictures on women: though they could not hold office as teachers in the public *synaxis* of the church, they possessed a sphere of "authority" in "the home" as "the teachers of virtue." The words of St Paul are clearly in Theodore's mind.

Another Antiochene teacher a generation later than Chrysostom was Theodoret, bishop of Cyrrhus. He was a great pastor and apologist, and he died about 457. In his *Commentary on 1 Corinthians,* at 1 Cor 11.9, he faithfully repeats the Pauline teaching about the subordination of women: "This is all that is needed to demonstrate the primacy of the man, for the

---

[7]Quoted in Peter Gorday, *Colossians, 1–2 Thessalonians, 1–2 Timothy, Titus, Philemon,* Ancient Christian Commentary on Scripture NT 9 (Downers Grove, Ill.: InterVarsity Press, 2000), 165.

woman was created to serve him, not the other way round."[8] He also writes in that commentary (on 1 Cor 11.8), "Man has the first place by order of creation."[9]

Another great pastor was St Epiphanius, bishop of Salamis in Cyprus. He is famous for his anti-heretical compendium *Panarion* (from the Latin "panarium," or "bread box," used as a chest for medicines against the poison of heresy)—for his quarrelling with St John Chrysostom. In that work, he speaks about a sect of women who had an exaggerated veneration of the Virgin Mary, the so-called Kollyridians (from the word for "bread rolls," which they ostensibly offered as a sacrifice in her name). Regarding them Epiphanius writes, "It is reported that certain women in Arabia have introduced this absurd teaching, how they offer up a sacrifice of bread rolls in the name of the ever-virgin [Mary] . . . in an unlawful and blasphemous ceremony, they ordain women, through whom they offer up the sacrifice in the name of Mary. This means that the entire proceeding is godless and sacrilegious, a perversion of the message of the Holy Spirit; in fact the whole thing is diabolical and a teaching of the impure spirit." (*Panarion*, 78.13) From these words, one might conclude that Epiphanius entertains a jaundiced view of the possible ordination of women, with the Marian component of the Kollyridians being the icing on the heretical cake. That conclusion would be correct. Later in the same work (79.3), he writes, "If women were to be charged by God with entering the priesthood or with assuming ecclesiastical office, then in the New Covenant it would have devolved upon no one more than Mary to fulfill a priestly function . . . But He did not find this good. Not even baptizing was entrusted to her." As far as the teacher of Cyprus is concerned, the ordination of women is an impossibility, and this is proven by the fact that not even one as worthy as the Mother of God was entrusted with any part of the priestly office. Not only did she not preside at the Eucharist, but she did not even baptize. All parts of the priestly office remain firmly closed to women. Epiphanius might have quarreled with Chrysostom, but he would have agreed with him about this: regarding the priesthood or ecclesiastical office, "the entire female sex must step back."

[8]Gerald Lewis Bray, *1–2 Corinthians*, Ancient Christian Commentary on Scripture NT 7 (Downers Grove, Ill.: InterVarsity Press, 1999), 108.
[9]Ibid.

One last reference may be looked at, that of "Ambrosiaster," the name now given to an anonymous Scripture commentator on the epistles of St Paul who wrote in the latter half of the fourth century. For a long time his work was wrongly attributed to St Ambrose (hence the name). In his work, he reflects the same admission of ontological equality and relational subordination as the other Christian writers we have considered: "Although man and woman are of the same substance, the man has relational priority because he is the head of the woman. He is greater than she is by cause and order, but not by substance. Woman is the glory of man, but there is an enormous distance between that and being the glory of God." Our author is careful to balance the equality and the subordination. Both genders share "the same substance." But the man is "greater" than the woman "by cause and order." Here the author reflects the Genesis stories. The man is the "cause" of the woman because she was taken from him, and he is greater in "order" because he preceded her so that she was made for him, and not *vice-versa*. Woman is thus "the glory of man"—of considerably less honor than the man, who is "the glory of God." We note that Ambrosiaster's understanding faithfully reflects that of St Paul, both in his assertion of women's "substantial" equality with men, as well as her subordination.

Reflections on the Patristic Material

In all the patristic material surveyed above (the tiniest taste out of the vast amount available) we see that the Fathers grasped the essential Scriptural teachings, that women were equal to men and also called to a subordinate position, especially in the Christian *synaxis*. That is, despite all the limitations which encumber interpreters in every age (including our own), the Fathers strove to be true to the Scriptural material. It will not do to write off their authority by saying that they "lived in a Late Antique culture where virtually everybody took male leadership in Church, family, and society for granted," or by dismissing views which take the Fathers seriously as "a conservative Protestant reading" of the Scriptures.[10] The

---

[10]Thus Nonna Verna Harrison, in her "Orthodox Arguments," in Thomas Hopko, ed., *Women and the Priesthood* (Crestwood, NY: St Vladimir's Seminary Press, 1999), 171.

Fathers indeed lived in a Late Antique culture, as we live in a secular, anti-Christian one. The question is whether or not, by reading the Scriptures, they had access to truth beyond the culture of their day. An Orthodox view of the Scriptures will confirm that they did.

For many modern interpreters of the Bible, the Scriptural material is diverse and of varied value. That is, some consider the first Genesis account (from the "E" or Elohist source) to be valuable, since it speaks of woman's equality with men, and the second Genesis account (from the "J" or Jahwist source) to be of considerably less value, since it reflects a more patriarchal view. Jesus, of course, is praised, since He valued women disciples as much as men. (His choice of all men for the Twelve is considered culturally accidental and of no significance.) The material in the epistles judged authentically Pauline (i.e., those which present an egalitarian view of gender) is accepted, while the material which asserts subordination is dismissed. That is, Scriptural material is considered piecemeal, and the authority of this or that piece is conditional upon its coinciding with our modern cultural norms. For the Fathers, however, it was otherwise: whatever variety the Scripture presented, they assumed its teaching formed one coherent whole, and that each piece of that whole had something valuable to contribute. All the various pieces were considered authoritative, since they were all Scripture. The author, style, nuance, and point to be made were all considered secondary. Between the feminist approach to Scripture and that of the Fathers, it seems "a great gulf is fixed"—so that "none (of the feminists) may cross from there to us."

In the opinion of these feminists, the Fathers' handling of the Scriptural material is anything but fair and even-handed. In their view, the Fathers gave lip-service to accepting the Scriptures which speak of women's equality with men, but what they gave with one hand, they took away with the other. That is, the only part of the Bible which really resonated for the Fathers and upon which they acted were the texts which speak of women's subordination, for if the Fathers really believed in the texts asserting feminine equality, they would have ordained women to the clerical office. This view of the Fathers, however, presupposes that the equality texts and the subordinationist texts stand in stark contradiction to one another—but the Fathers were prevented from holding such a presupposition by their view that all parts of Scripture were authoritative. For the Fathers, these sets of texts contained no inherent contradiction: a woman could regard herself as the equal of her husband and yet still follow his leadership. How such a combination might be possible will be the focus of our next chapter.

CHAPTER 4

The Leadership of Men

I am aware that by using the term "subordination" throughout this book to describe the wife's relation to her husband, I use what some may consider inflammatory language. Scriptural terms like "submission" (1 Cor 14.34, Eph 5.22ff, Col 3.18, 1 Pt 3.5) or "headship" (1 Cor 11.3, Eph 5.23) or describing woman as "the weaker vessel" (1 Pt 3.7) do not sit well with us egalitarian moderns. In the words of one author, they "lead many readers today to cringe."[1] That is because the words today are heard by a culture struggling to eliminate genuine injustices done to women, and it seems as if these words support the culture and patterns of injustice against which they are struggling. These words, once spoken in a time when they were not considered inflammatory or controversial, are now uttered in the midst of that struggle, and so they possess a far harsher sound than they did originally. I could find gentler words, or more politically correct terms. In the title of this chapter, I use the term "leadership" rather than headship. But the issue is not resolved by changing terms, but by examining what the terms actually mean and how such leadership is meant to function. It is important to reiterate that much of the feminist struggle is something the Church can and should support. By defending the Scriptural and patristic views on the subordination of women, I am not thereby taking sides against the legitimate aspirations of women. I am, however, saying the Church should not ordain women to authoritative church office such as deacon, presbyter, or bishop.[2]

---

[1]Bouteneff, op. cit., 52.

[2]Establishing such an order of women priests would, I suggest, certainly result in schism within the Orthodox world. This is implicitly acknowledged by Behr-Sigel in her plaintive call for "a disciplinary pluralism," wherein some Orthodox churches ordain women while others do not (*Ministry*, op. cit., 179). It is, I submit, supremely unlikely that the intro-

The Typological Model

How to begin defending the biblical and patristic tradition of the leadership of men in family and church structure? Perhaps one could begin by re-examining the image in Ephesians 5.28–32. In this passage, the author refers to Genesis 2.24, which declares that "a man shall leave his father and mother and shall cleave to his wife and the two shall become one flesh." He then asserts that this is a "great *mystērion*," a revelation for the initiated Christian, and that it refers "to Christ and His Church." The author is reading the entire Old Testament with reference to Christ, and with the conviction that faith in Christ now lights up and brings out the deeper meaning in all the old Scriptures. Prior to Christ, Jews read this Genesis text about the husband and wife becoming one flesh as simply being about a matrimonial reality. But now that we have experienced Christ's love and our intimate union with Him (so that we are "one spirit" with Him, 1 Cor 6.17), we read this Genesis text with new eyes. Specifically, we see that the deep communion and one-flesh reality of marriage not only prefigure the union of Christ with His Church—they have their original source in that union.

I would suggest that this union provides a key to understanding the marriage relationship and love generally. For example, in the *Song of Solomon*, we see the erotic love between man and woman. But older interpreters were not wrong to see in it also the eternal love of God for His people, nor the mystics the love of God for the human soul. Of course it is referring to human love, but this human love is rooted in the divine. As C.S. Lewis writes, "[To say that the *Song of Solomon* is about Christ and His Church] is not arbitrary, and springs from depths I had not suspected . . . the language of nearly all great mystics . . . confronts us with evidence that the image of marriage, of sexual union, is not only profoundly natural but almost inevitable as a means of expressing the desired union between God and man . . . for the mystics God is the Bridegroom of the individual soul."[3] The unsuspected "depths" of which Lewis speaks are the eternal

duction of women priests would be tolerated in Orthodoxy as a legitimate disciplinary pluralism.

[3]C.S. Lewis, *Reflections on the Psalms* (London: Fontana Books, 1961), 108. Bobrinskoy agrees, saying, "woman herself becomes the symbol of the believing soul" (op. cit., 223).

love of God for His creation. The love between husband and wife provides the imagery for the love between God and us because God's love is the primordial source of that love.

God's love is the original, ours is the derivative. It was not the case that our human love for one another came first and that we then said by way of metaphor and analogy that God relates to us in the same way. Rather, His love came first, in eternity and in His plan for created human nature, and human love came later as the pale reflection and manifestation of it. In the same way, Christ's eternal love for His Church is the pattern, the *typos*, the type. (A Platonist would describe it as a "Form," an "Idea.") Before Man and Woman were created, Christ knew and planned His saving love for His Church (even as His sacrifice on the cross was foreknown from the foundation of the world; 1 Pt 2.19–20), and the creation of Adam and Eve and of marriage was ordered after that eternal *typos*. The love of every husband for his wife is patterned after it. If I had to describe the case for the leadership of men, I would therefore describe it as "typological."

The husband exercises the leadership in his relationship with his wife because Christ is the Leader of His Church, and the wife submits to him (or if you like, "follows his lead") because the Church follows the leadership of Christ. Abusive husbands have unhappily made the idea of male leadership a "hard sell" for some. There seems to be no shortage of men who have no idea what true Christian authority or headship looks like, but who nonetheless quote the biblical texts in order to justify their abuse and domination of their wives. But the misuse does not cancel the proper use, nor invalidate the Scriptural model. To see what real leadership looks like, according to our typological argument, we need to look to Christ, to see how He relates to *His* bride. And we see that, far from dominating and abusing her, He "gave Himself up for her" (Eph 5.25), dying to His own will on the cross for her that He might make her glorious. The call to lead is a call to die to self for the other.

This typological understanding therefore sees the Man and Woman as earthly fulfillments of Christ and His Church, so that the characteristics of Christ and His Church are meant to characterize husband and wife also. Christ and His church are the "types," the patterns (Greek=*typos*); husband and wife are the "antitypes," the fulfillments (Greek=*antitypos*). In this typology Christ is *active*, taking action to save His bride; the Church is *receptive*, receiving His salvation as the free gift of grace. Christ is *the seeker*, leaving the high halls of heaven to pursue His bride, even to "the lower parts of the earth" (Eph 4.9); the Church is *the sought* whom the bridegroom comes to find. Christ is *the lover* who pours out His love to save the life of His bride; the Church is *the beloved* who accepts His love and is brought to life. These typological characteristics are to be imitated in married love by the man and woman also: the man is the active, the seeker, the lover; the woman is receptive, the sought, the beloved. The man is to enact the role of the eternal masculine. He images the divine life-giver, the Sky-Father. The woman enacts the role of the eternal feminine, and images the created life-bearer, the Earth-Mother. Gender was created to be freighted with this typological significance, to express the song of creation, the saving dialogue and union between Creator and creation, between Christ and His Church. Paganism had faint adumbrations of this dialogue and union, with its myths of Sky-Father and Earth-Mother. These shadows found reality in Christ and His people, and are embodied (literally) in the union of husband and wife. As Lewis writes about marital *eros* in his book *The Four Loves*, "In the act of love we are not merely ourselves. We are also representatives. . . . In us all the masculinity and femininity of the world, all that is assailant and responsive, are momentarily focused."[4] St Gregory of Nyssa may have thought that God's original blueprint for the creation of men and women was to be in the genderless image of God, with gender differentiation being a secondary development, and not in the best "blueprint."[5] With all due respect to the great Cappadocian, I suggest that this gender differentiation is precisely in the original blueprint, and that it is there to express the eternal realities of Christ and His Church.[6] This does not mean, let us hasten to add, that the husband is somehow more "divine" or closer to God than the wife. To

---

[4]C.S. Lewis, *The Four Loves* (London: Fontana Books, 1960), 95.

[5]Bouteneff speaks of God adding sex distinction to humanity "which otherwise would have remained '*purely*' in his image" op. cit., 159 (italics mine).

[6]Cf. John Behr, "The Rational Animal: A Rereading of Gregory of Nyssa's *De hominis opificio*" *Journal of Early Christian Studies* 7.2 (Summer 1999): 219–247. In this eye-opening article, Fr John presents an analysis that overturns the usual reading of a "double creation" in St Gregory's treatise.

say this would be to mistake the role for the reality. The husband plays in the marriage the role of the Sky-Father, and the wife the role of the Earth-Mother. At the end of it all, both players know that they are human, and not divine—and that they are ontologically part of the creation, the Earth-Mother. As the mystics would remind them if they forget, all souls, both of men and women, are feminine before God. Husband and wife both are part of the Bride of Christ. We describe the typology they embody and enact, not their ontological reality.

Further, one should not press this typology beyond its proper sphere—it is about our inter-relationships as husband and wife, the elegant, stylized waltz performed jointly by the leader and the led, not about our precise biology. Biology does not know the degree of purity that typology can know. One can have a purely masculine "*type*," but one's *biology* cannot be purely masculine, one with no trace of the feminine. Obviously men have female hormones and women have male hormones. And everyone knows of somewhat effeminate men and somewhat masculine women, whether these are hormonally caused or not. But these biological details do not invalidate the basic truth of the typology—that men and women are different, and these differences are not confined to the purely anatomical. If the difference in roles were rooted in biology, then these hormonal nuances would be a problem, but the difference is not rooted in the phenomenology of our physical existence, but in Christ and His Church. Our different biology, anatomy, and the physics of our different sexuality may *witness* to this difference in roles, but they are not solely the *source* of it.

This typological model finds expression also in the liturgical life of the Church. The pastor, whether priest or bishop, is an image of God. That is, all the People of God receive the sacramental mysteries from God, though the mouth which pronounces the saving sacramental words and the hand which performs the sacramental action be that of the priest. The priest, therefore, functions as an icon of God. It is not simply that the priest exercises in the congregation a fatherly authority, consistent with that of a father within the family. That is true, but there is more. It is also that the priest images and represents the saving Divine within the Church, and is a sacramental presence of it.[7]

[7] As Hopko has well said, "As God the Father is the father of those who become his

Confirmation of the pastor as an icon of God's authority is also found in what some might consider an unlikely place: the Book of Revelation. In Revelation 4, we see an image of God (i.e., God the Father; Christ the Son comes before us in Revelation 5, as the Lamb), sitting upon a throne and surrounded twenty-four elders (Greek=*presbyteroi*, presbyters). Any Christian from the early centuries would have instantly recognized in this vision the liturgical arrangements of his or her own Sunday Eucharist, for there the bishop sat on his throne, surrounded by his presbyters. God enthroned with His heavenly "presbyters" is thus reflected in the life of the Church, where the bishop is liturgically enthroned with his presbyters. Here we see clearly how the pastor (that is, the bishop or, as today, the local presbyter) functions as an icon of God. And this saving divine Presence is masculine—not male (all acknowledge that God has no gender), but masculine.

It is important to recognize this reality, and not to lose sight of it through the complementary recognition that God has no body and therefore no gender. For masculinity and femininity, in the typological modes that we have been considering, are not confined to gender. Masculinity is not confined to maleness. Yahweh, though not a male, is still masculine; He is a god, not a goddess.[8] The pagan gods often had their consorts, for those gods were representations and embodiments of the forces of fertility within nature. It was thus inevitable that they therefore were imaged as both gods and goddesses, and served on earth by both priests and priestesses. But, whatever early developments in the religion of Israel may have been,[9] our Scriptures teach that Yahweh was transcendent above the forces of nature, since He was the Creator of nature. He therefore had, and could have, no consort. There could be no "Mrs. Yahweh," completing His maleness with Her femaleness, and mirroring the earthly natural fertility wherein a male must have his female to be complete. As

children by becoming members of Christ, so the married man is to be the father of his family's children, and the presbyter/bishop the father of the members of his church." Thomas Hopko, "Presbyter/Bishop: A Masculine Ministry," in Thomas Hopko, ed., *Women and the Priesthood* (Crestwood, NY: St Vladimir's Seminary Press, 1999), 158.

[8]This is, I suggest, the reason that the priesthood in Israel was closed to women and that their God was not served by priestesses as well as priests.

[9]See the works of Margaret Barker for an attempt to reconstruct the pre-exilic cult.

transcendent above all nature, Yahweh was, and must be, masculine, for masculinity typologically images the active, not the passive, the original, not the derivative. Nature is passive, since it was created. Nature is derivative, since it finds its origin in God. It is thus feminine. We properly speak of "Mother Nature," not "Father Nature." Our God, Father, Son, and Holy Spirit, is thus masculine, even if transcending maleness. Attempts to evade this by citing feminine metaphors for God are futile.[10] The Father of our Lord Jesus Christ remains relentlessly masculine.

This is the typological significance of the liturgical priesthood, since the priest images this masculine God. To deny this and to assert that a woman could be a priest would be to assert also that the priest has no iconic significance, and does not in fact image this masculine God. Or, conversely, it is to assert that the Deity imaged by the priest/priestess is not such a God, but could equally well be spoken of as a Goddess, as our Mother in heaven as well as our Father in heaven.[11] Such assertions strike at the heart of all Orthodox liturgical experience. And as C.S. Lewis said, if such were the case, "it is an argument not in favor of Christian priestesses but against Christianity"[12]—or at least against Orthodox Christianity as liturgically expressed and experienced from its inception. For all of our liturgical experience reveals that the priest/bishop images and manifests God in our midst—the God who is relentlessly masculine, who pursues His bride even at the cost of His own death and beyond, who betroths her to Himself, and who protects and cares for her, even as an earthly husband does his wife.

---

[10]For example, Is 49.15 is sometimes cited as evidence of the maternal in Yahweh: "Can a woman forget her sucking child, that she should have no compassion on the son of her womb? Even these may forget, yet I will not forget you." Yet in this passage, Yahweh is not compared to a mother, but *contrasted* with one—His love surpasses even that of mothers. Compare the comments of John Oswalt on the passage in his *The Book of Isaiah, Chapters 44–66* (Grand Rapids, MI: Eerdmans, 1998), 305–306.

[11]This was recognized by C.S. Lewis in his essay in 1948, "Priestesses in the Church?," in Walter Hooper, ed., *God in the Dock* (Grand Rapids, MI: 1970), 234–239.

[12]Ibid.

Male Leadership in the Family

These typological roles are also manifested in the family. Though husband and wife each enact a role in imaging the eternal realities of Christ and His Church, the parts are not arbitrarily assigned, for men and women have physical and psychological differences that equip them to play their roles. Physically, the man's anatomy leads him to fatherhood, and the woman's to motherhood, and once they become parents, differing tasks are required of each. That is, the mother takes time to nurse and nurture the newborns, while the father classically provides the necessary food and shelter. And it is not just in their outward anatomy that man and woman are different. Psychologically, the "inner anatomy" is different too. As a popular writer said, "Men are from Mars, women are from Venus."[13] The genders have different ways of processing information and experiencing reality,[14] and it is in the combining and uniting of these differences that love and mutual self-sacrifice are made possible. We love the other not because the other is the same as us, because precisely because the other is different. Men and women find these inner differences not only frustrating, but (paradoxically) delightful. Each *wants* the other to be different internally, to delight in different things. It is in these differences that each can enrich the other.

These basic psychological differences contribute to the differing roles man and woman play in the family—that is, the roles of father and mother. The father's role is fundamentally different from the mother's role, and both are equally important for the raising of children (just as both are physically required to have children in the first place). Brook Herbert, in her brilliant essay, "Towards a Recovery of the Theology of Patriarchy,"[15] speaks of motherhood as reflecting "a specific posture between a woman and her child consonant with feminine sexuality," and fatherhood (or "patriarchy"

---

[13] John Gray, *Men are from Mars, Women are from Venus* (New York, NY: Harper Collins, 1992).

[14] See the book *Brain Sex* by Anne Moir and David Jessel (New York, NY: Bantam, Doubleday, Dell, 1989). Also, as Behr-Sigel says, "men and women have different ways of being in the world," op. cit., 131.

[15] "Towards a Recovery of the Theology of Patriarchy," *St Vladimir's Theological Quarterly*, 40.4 (1996): 287–301.

as she calls it) as reflecting "not sexual priority and dominance but the relational posture of father to child consonant with masculine sexuality."[16] Herbert builds on the book *Flight from Woman* by psychiatrist Karl Stern, and observes that the masculine mode of perception is that of "discursive reasoning," while feminine perception "demonstrates a predominantly intuitive, holistic and empathetic thrust."[17] This does not deny that "both modes may coexist within an individual," but it does mean that there is a "persistent continuity of sexual roles evident pan-culturally and trans-historically—the broad sweep of human experience wherein men and women behave differently."[18] In other words, one consistently sees that fathers and mothers relate to their children differently, the fathers acting as men and tending to external objectivity and mothers acting as women and tending to greater intuitiveness.

Part of this talent for the external in fathers involves the encounter with the child as outsider and welcoming of the child into the family. To quote Herbert again at length:

> Initially, fatherhood represents an objective encounter between two uniquely distinct individuals. Standing outside the child, the father's reception of the infant into the world constitutes the formatively significant legitimization of the child's being. . . . Because the father stands 'outside' the child, this primary reception constitutes the child's welcome into the external cosmos—authenticating through his own stance as protector and guardian the child's very 'right' to exist; his inclusion in the cosmic sphere. . . . The father also stands between the family unit and the world as mediator and authority . . . [These functions of legitimization and mediation are not] exclusively the prerogative of the father. Rather all is accomplished within the relational unity of father and mother. . . . But within the family it is the posture of the father, as affirming and loving presence overarching the family, that circumscribes the protection and nurture of each person.[19]

[16]Ibid., 294.
[17]Ibid., 296, 295.
[18]Ibid., 296.
[19]Ibid., 297–8.

Here we see the man's role as father within the family, consistent with his masculinity, which could be summed up as welcoming the "outsider" (in this case, the newborn) into the family, and protecting the family by acting as mediating liaison between the family and the outer world. The woman's role within the family is different, and is consistent with her feminine gifts of intuition and empathy. The father allows the family to exist by legitimizing its new members and protecting it from outside threat. The mother makes this family a place of beauty, peace, and growth. Both gifts and contributions are needed. Again, this does not mean that women cannot reason discursively or that men cannot empathize. But it does posit in general (in Herbert's words) "a persistent continuity of sexual roles." Each parent has characteristic strengths that the other needs if the family is to be holy and healthy.

The Role of the Pastor in the Church Family

With regard to ordination to the pastoral office, we note that the gifts required for pastor in the church community are precisely those of the father in the family. The very term "*presbyteros*," presbyter, elder, refers back to this role of governing authority, for the "elders" in the Jewish community (the origin of the New Testament term) were figures who ruled. That indeed is how Paul characterizes the task of presbyters—those who "rule," "direct," "manage" (Greek=*proistēmi*). Thus the bishop (*episcopos*) is to "rule his own household well," for "if a man does not know how to rule his own household, how will he take care of the church of God?" (1 Tim 3.4–5). Thus elders/*presbyteroi* are to "rule well" (1 Tim 5.17). This governing function is also seen in the title "shepherd" (Greek=*poimēn*), for to "shepherd" the flock is to rule it. This is apparent from the translation[20] of (for example) Revelation 2.27: Christ will "rule the nations with a rod of iron," the word rendered "to rule" being the Greek *poimainō*, "to shepherd." Thus though presbyters and shepherds are called to counsel, heal, preach, offer the Eucharist, and do many other things, their main task is ruling.

---

[20]Rendered thus by AV, RSV, NEB, NASB, NAB, TEV, and others.

What does this function of ruling involve? For the answer, let us look at the ordination prayer for the bishop (who in the early Church functioned as the head pastor and liturgical celebrant) and for the presbyter.

The present Byzantine ordination prayer for bishops reads in part: "Make this man also who has been proclaimed a steward of the episcopal grace, to be an imitator of You, the true Shepherd who laid down Your life for Your sheep; to be a leader of the blind, a light to those in darkness, a reprover of the foolish, a teacher of the young, a lamp to the world." We see that most of the prayer is devotional, not descriptive—it encourages the new bishop to take his pastoral duties seriously in preaching the Gospel to all.

The ordination for bishops in the third century found in Hippolytus' *Apostolic Tradition* is more descriptive. It reads in part: "Bestow upon this Your servant whom You have chosen for the episcopate, to shepherd Your holy flock and to serve You as high-priest, blamelessly liturgizing[21] night and day; to propitiate Your countenance unceasingly and to offer You the gifts of Your holy church; and by the high-priestly spirit to have authority to forgive sins according to Your command; to ordain [literally "to give lots," Greek *didonai klērous*) according to Your bidding; to loose every bond according to the power which You gave to the apostles."

In this second prayer we can detect a kind of job description for bishops—i.e., for pastors, since the bishop was the local pastor at the time this prayer was written. In particular, the bishop's liturgical job was:

1) to offer the Eucharist as the main presider ("offer You the gifts of Your holy Church")

2) to reconcile the excommunicated to the communion of the Church through confession ("to forgive sins according to Your command" (Jn 20.23);

3) to ordain deacons, presbyters, and other clergy ("to give *klērous*, i.e., to ordain);

4) to exorcize and heal ("to loose every bond according to the power given to the apostles" (Mt 10.1).

[21]That is, offering the Eucharistic Liturgy.

The present Byzantine ordination prayer for presbyters reads in part: "Fill this man with the gift of Your Holy Spirit that he may be worthy to stand in innocence before Your altar; to proclaim the Gospel of Your Kingdom; to minister the Word of Your truth; to offer to You spiritual gifts and sacrifices; to renew Your people through the washing of rebirth." When we compare these functions with those of the bishop in the third century as found in the *Apostolic Tradition*, we see that in the time between then and now, the bishops and presbyters have largely traded functions. Or, more precisely, most of the bishop's local pastoral functions have devolved upon the presbyters. This is inevitable, since the size of the bishops' diocese has increased dramatically so that the bishop is no longer able to act as the main pastor through all his diocese, and must rely upon his fellow-presbyters. We see in this present Byzantine prayer that the pastor's job description includes:

1) to preside at liturgical services ("to stand before Your altar");

2) to preach ("to proclaim the gospel of Your Kingdom");

3) to preside at the Eucharist ("to offer to You spiritual gifts and sacrifices");

4) to baptize ("to renew Your people through the washing of rebirth").

The ordination for bishops in the third century found in Hippolytus' *Apostolic Tradition* for presbyters is more succinct, since in his day the bishop was the main pastor. The presbyters' main task (there was a plurality of them surrounding their bishop as a kind of "board") is to help rule and govern, making the day-to-day decisions about who would be ordained, reconciled, etc. The relevant bit of the ordination prayer reads: "Fill him with the Spirit of grace and counsel that he may share in the presbyterate and govern Your people with a pure heart." We see from this prayer that the main function of the presbyter of the third century was to share in the ruling and governing of the Church.

The Scriptures speak of the task of the *episcopos/presbyteros* (i.e., bishop/presbyter—the terms were used interchangeably then; compare

Acts 20.17, 28 and Titus 1.5, 7) as one of ruling. From these prayers, we can gain a more detailed understanding of what this ruling entails: baptizing, presiding at the Eucharist, preaching, reconciling the penitent. All of these functions involve the exercise of authority. Baptizing involves authority because it brings in the outsider, declaring him or her to be now a part of the Church. Presiding at the Eucharist involves authority, since the celebrant presides by virtue of his role as head of the community. Preaching involves authority, since it is not simply the offering of helpful advice, but the declaration of the Church's teaching, the time when the preacher "rightly defines the Word of God's truth." Reconciling the penitent involves authority, since, like baptism, it involves bringing an excommunicate "outsider" once more into the church community.

We see in these pastoral functions of the priest to his congregation the father's functioning in his family with his children. As the father "legitimizes" the newborn children by accepting and protecting them, so the pastor "legitimizes" the place of the newly baptized (and formerly excommunicated) through baptism (and confession/absolution). As the father forms the liaison between his family and the outside world, so the pastor, and especially the bishop, forms the link between the local congregation and the other churches and Christian communities. In the case of the bishop, this means that the community/diocese/parish under him finds its link to the rest of world Orthodoxy through its Eucharistic communion with him. By being in communion with the bishop, the local believer is in communion with the rest of the Orthodox Church.

Obviously today the busy pastor does more than the tasks described in the ordination prayers. There is the phone to answer, counseling to give, prayers to offer in private, meetings to chair, and so on and so forth. But administrative and therapeutic tasks do not embody the heart of the pastoral office. The essential and defining tasks of the pastoral office are summed up in the ordination prayers—and it is just these prayers which express the masculine role of father within the family.[22]

Ultimately, the priest is more than the sum of his tasks. Priesthood is not what he *does*; it is what he *is*—just as a father within a family is not

---

[22]Cf. Thomas Hopko, "Presbyter/Bishop: A Masculine Ministry," in Thomas Hopko, ed., *Women in the Priesthood* (Crestwood, NY: St Vladimir's Seminary Press, 1999), 139–164.

someone who does this or that job, but someone who *is*, who embodies the fatherhood of God in and for the family. From much feminist writing, one gains the impression that the priesthood is a career—a holy career, to be sure, but ultimately a career, and as such, is adequately described only in terms of function (which is how some men model it to the world). A woman can preach as well as a man; she can counsel as well as a man; etc. If she can do the job, why then can she not have the office? But the priesthood is *not* in fact a career and cannot adequately be described in terms of function anymore than fatherhood can. The priest is the father to the church family, an image (or better, an icon) of God the Father, manifesting the divine authority and love in the church even as the father does in his family. As Herbert says, "a transfigured ordained priesthood exists solely as love and familial commitment. It is a manifestation of 'fatherhood' . . . expressed in the motion of reciprocal love between priest congregation . . . a male priesthood expresses the positive and life-affirming role of fatherhood."[23] Women have many gifts, but are incapable of imaging the divine Fatherhood through their earthly fatherhood, since the feminine (to quote Herbert once again) reflects "a specific posture between a woman and her child consonant with feminine sexuality."[24] In a word, women cannot be priests, because priests are fathers. A priest is primarily a representative. To declare gender irrelevant would mean to make that representation aniconic, without iconic significance, and miss the whole point. A man can represent God the Father to his family precisely because he is a father. The iconic significance is central to the role.

Priest as Icon of Christ?

The iconic significance of which I am speaking is different from that suggested by such writers as Bobrinskoy. In his book *The Mystery of the Church*, he speaks of the celebrant as "an icon of Christ and of the Community,"[25] and asserts that the priest represents both Christ and the Church. The priest therefore partakes of both feminine elements (when he represents the Church, the bride of Christ), and masculine ones (when he represents

[23]Herbert, op. cit., 300. Herbert is, of course, expressing the intended ideal.
[24]Herbert, op. cit., 294.
[25]Bobrinskoy, op. cit., 224.

Christ). As the Church is both feminine and masculine, both the bride and the body of Christ, so the priest also embodies these twin elements. "When the celebrant ... is turned toward the East ... he is then like the Bride standing face to face with the Lord. ... When the one presiding ... is no longer turned toward the East, but toward the people ... then he is acting *in persona Christi*. ... Here we can point to the iconic nature of the priest's maleness."[26] "It is in Christ's maleness that the priest's male identity has its grounding."[27] For Bobrinskoy, the priest's maleness is part of his ability fittingly to represent Christ.

The argument which grounds the male character of the ministerial priesthood in Christ's maleness has been examined at length by Metropolitan Kallistos Ware.[28] In this examination, Ware argues that Christ's maleness has little to do with His priesthood, and that therefore the maleness of the priest is not required for him to represent Christ. Christ functions as our heavenly high-priest because He became *anthrōpos*, not because He became *anēr*. His maleness, while not devoid of significance (can anything about Christ be devoid of significance?), is not crucial to His priesthood. Ware rightly points out that the Fathers seem little concerned about Christ's maleness, and even their writings on the Feast of Christ's Circumcision, where one might expect such themes, stress His divine condescension, and not the significance of His masculinity. Ware also argues that the priest, while in some sense representing Christ (it is through the priest's liturgizing ministry that Christ is sacramentally present), does not in fact speak "*in persona Christi*, but *in persona Ecclesiae*."[29] In the Anaphora, he does not recite the Words of Institution as if he were Christ Himself, but rather "acting in union with the people and in their name, he recites the *epiclesis*. ... At this crucial moment ... he is not Christ's vicar or icon, but—in union with the people—he stands as a supplicant before God."[30]

---

[26]Bobrinskoy, op. cit., 224–225.

[27]Bobrinskoy, op. cit., 230.

[28]In his "Man, Woman and the Priesthood of Christ" in Thomas Hopko, ed., *Women and the Priesthood* (Crestwood, NY: St Vladimir's Seminary Press, 1999).

[29]Ware, op. cit., 47.

[30]Ibid., 48.

I find Ware's argumentation convincing. Especially significant is his observation that the "iconic argument" that a priest must be male because Christ was male is "essentially a new argument, developed in the second half of the twentieth century but not explicit in earlier Tradition."[31] The Fathers did not make this argument when they argued against the possibility of women priests, nor is the iconic argument rooted in the Scriptures.

In fact, the New Testament, as we have seen, does not refer to the *episcopos* or the *presbyteros* in priestly terms at all. Rather, the concept of Christian priesthood is found in only two *loci*—that of the heavenly ministry of Christ, and that of the liturgical character of His earthly Church, the royal priesthood. The Church is said to be a holy and royal priesthood, offering spiritual sacrifices (1 Pt 2.5, 8). Its sharing with the poor, its works of *diakonia*, are said to be "sacrifices pleasing to God" (Heb 13.16). It is true that, in Romans 15.15–16, Paul speaks of his own ministry in priestly terms, since he is a *leitourgos* of Christ, offering priestly service (=*ierourgeō*) to God. Paul is speaking, however, not of his liturgizing or presiding at the Church's *synaxis*, but of his ministry of preaching and of converting the Gentiles. His point is that he is writing to his hearers (in this case, the Romans) so that they may be sanctified, since Paul's task is to offer them as *prosphora* acceptable to God, sanctified by the Holy Spirit. Here again the priestly reality is found primarily in the Church as a whole, and not in the persons of its clergy. As seen above, the clergy are described in the New Testament primarily in terms of rule, not of liturgical function. The term "priest" (=*iereus*) is never used to describe them.

What we do find in the Scriptures and in the Fathers is a concept of Eucharist as sacrifice. Paul compares the *trapeza* of the Lord to the altar of Israel, and contrasts it with the *trapeza* of the pagan sacrifices (1 Cor 10.18–21), clearly implying that the Eucharist is sacrificial. The *Didache* refers in 14.1 to the Eucharist as "your sacrifice" (=*thysia*). Clement, writing around the same time at the end of the first century, in his *Letter to the Corinthians* 44:4 and 36:1, speaks of the bishops as those who "offer the gifts" (=*prosenegkontas ta dōra*), so that Christ is the "high priest of our offerings" (=*archierea tōn prosphorōn ēmōn*). A patristic commonplace

[31] Ibid., 41.

identifies the Eucharist with the pure offering prophesied in Malachi 1.11. Though the clergy are primarily rulers—Clement refers to them in 21.6 as those who guide, who go before to show the way (=*proēgeomai*)—one of their tasks as rulers is presiding at the Eucharist, the Church's sacrifice. The bishop/presbyter presides at the Eucharist for the same reason that a father is the one who "says grace" with his family at meal time—because he is the head of the family. From this it is but a short (and not inappropriate) step to describe the presiding cleric as a priest, since he is the one who offers the Church's sacrifice.[32]

We now tend to think of presbyters primarily as those who liturgize, who perform the liturgical services, and because of that liturgical function, as men who also head up the community (perhaps under the watchful supervision of church boards). In the New Testament and the early Church, it was otherwise and opposite: bishops/presbyters were primarily those who headed the community and ruled it, and because of this rule, were those who also liturgized. Indeed, as we have seen, one of the classic ordination prayers for presbyters makes no mention of liturgizing at all, but simply of his function of governing ("Fill him with the Spirit of grace and counsel that he may share in the presbyterate and govern Your people with a pure heart").

I would therefore suggest that presbyters are primarily rulers, that ministerial priesthood (which is but one aspect of the total ministry of presbyters), though real and effective, is a derived priesthood, one that is rooted in the corporate priesthood of the church as a whole—which corporate priesthood is itself a reflection and manifestation of the heavenly priesthood of Christ. That is, a presbyter is a priest because he embodies, and speaks for, and rules the priestly people of God, not because he immediately represents Christ as His icon or vicar or intermediary. The priestly aspect of his ministry comes from Christ, of course, but *through* the people. Certainly, the priest in one way immediately represents Christ, in that he manifests His ruling authority (cf. Lk 10.16: "he who hears you, hears Me"). But this immediate and iconic representation is one of author-

---

[32]The term "priest" was originally attached to bishops, not presbyters, since bishops were the original presidents at the Eucharist, that function only later devolving more characteristically on the presbyters.

ity, not priesthood. His ministerial priesthood (though not his ministerial authority) is derived from the Church. This does not make the priest simply the delegate of the people, since (as Ware himself points out[33] and as we have said), his ruling authority comes directly from Christ. He stands with them, as part of the *laos*, and over them, as their ruler. His priesthood, however, his ability to liturgize, is rooted in the priesthood of the entire priestly people. If this strikes us as strange, it is perhaps because we have de-sanctified the laity[34] and no longer view them as priestly.

The presbyter is an icon, therefore, not so much of Christ our High Priest, as of divine rule and fatherhood, in that the presbyter's task is to manifest that fatherhood, the spiritual authority which governs, defines, and protects. Presbyters must be men, because gender is not irrelevant to fatherhood.

Echoes of Male Leadership in Contemporary Culture

It is one thing to assert the truth of the typological model we have been discussing, and quite another to prove it. Indeed, some feminist writers would object as we emerge from the very starting gate of the argument, and say that it is not valid to base the typological argument against women priests on Ephesians 5.28–32, because the author of the epistle is tainted with unacceptable patriarchy to begin with. His concern, say the objectors, is to subordinate women to their husbands, and the author of the epistle simply drags in the Christ–Church analogy to justify the oppression. No argument could be based upon it that today's feminists would find acceptable and convincing.

There is much merit to this objection. In the debate over the ordination of women to the priesthood, it sometimes seems like the two partners in the debate are hopelessly at odds, since they have contradictory first principles. For those who reject the ordination of women, the authority of Scripture is a first principle, and no amount of argument based on the concept of "rights" will convince them to deny the teaching of Scripture. For those who advocate the ordination of women, the concept of equal

---

[33]Op. cit., 44.

[34]For one to say today, "I'm a layman in these matters" is to confess oneself uneducated and uninitiated; whereas in the New Testament, the *laos* were precisely the initiated.

rights is a first principle, and no amount of proof-texting will convince them that the denial of that right is justified. Of course one cannot argue *to* first principles, but only *from* first principles. That is what the term "first principles" means. Is there nothing outside these two conflicting "first principles" that can speak to the debate?

I think there is: love poetry, fairy-tales, and the convictions of children. (G.K. Chesterton would, I think, agree: he once wrote in his book *Orthodoxy,* in the chapter "The Ethics of Elfland," "I left the fairy tales lying on the floor of the nursery, and I have not found any books so sensible since."[35])

The convictions of children witness to the fundamental difference between father and mother, between man and woman, and we can discern in these convictions echoes of the typology we have been discussing. I remember how once a child fell into distress—it was a minor distress, and one that afflicts young toddlers every other day or so: he fell off his tricycle and sustained a cut and a bruise. It was nothing, of course, but for the toddler it was a catastrophe of cosmic proportions, and one that needed immediate emergency care. The accident happened five feet from the father, but he was of no help. Without stopping to consider, the child ran tearfully past the father to seek out the mother. The father later confessed to me that he felt somewhat distressed himself at being so utterly invisible and useless in his child's eyes. But the child knew that what was required to set his universe right was not a father. The child instinctively sought (in Herbert's words) "a specific posture . . . consonant with feminine sexuality"—that is, a mother, because mothers are persons of "intuitive, holistic, and empathetic thrust." Other situations require other remedies. When the child is frightened of robbers, spiders, or space-aliens in the closet, they cry out for the father, because fathers are persons who stand at the gate, keeping out what should remain outside and thus protecting those within.

The convictions of children find echo also in fairy-tales. In fairy-tales, we see displayed the true and transcendent relations between man and woman, the underlying mythology of healthy humanity. There the man is

[35]David Dooley, ed., *The Collected Works of G.K. Chesterton,* vol. 1 (San Francisco: Ignatius Press, 1986), 249–268.

the knight in shining armour, the woman the fair damsel. He is called to do battle for her, protecting her honor with life and limb, going on quests, slaying dragons, carrying her token on his person as he rides into danger. It is easy to smile or mock the idealism of chivalry (especially now when the symbolism of chivalrous ages is foreign to our culture), but the tales retain their potency for the human heart nonetheless. I submit that each woman wants her man to be her knight in shining armour, and each man wants to look upon his woman as his fair damsel, his noble and beautiful lady. Advancing old age, the wear and tear of daily life, and the cynicism spawned by our culture of divorce may mock the vision. But the vision remains the true one, and the human heart is the poorer when it denies it, and settles for something less.

The vision's veracity, the proof of the paradigm it offers, is confirmed by love poetry, and in the behavior of men and women when they are in love. The love poetry to which I refer does not simply refer to the traditions of Christianity. The typological binary *personas* of seeker-sought, lover-beloved, wooer-wooed find expressions in all the great traditions of human culture. These fundamental roles for the genders are rooted in the human psyche, the human heart, and are trans-cultural.

When a man is in love with a woman, the true and transcendent nature of male headship is revealed. This headship has nothing whatsoever to do with domination. Some dark forms of lust have to do with domination, but these are a thousand miles away from the heart that is in love. Indeed, lust and love are opposites, for love is the great conqueror of lust. A man in love brings the beloved flowers, writes the beloved poetry (or reads it to her), delights in the bows of gallantry and the heroism of quests. He wants to discover what she wants so that he can give it to her. If there is danger, he stands to protect her from it. The idea of responding to a common threat (for example, the possibility of a burglar in the house) by sending her to meet it is repugnant—not just to his male pride, but to his love for her. It is *he* that abases himself for *her*, not *vice-versa*: *he* proposes marriage to *her* on bended knee, and he knows instinctively that the opposite—her proposing to him on bended knee—is an outrage. True headship, true masculine love, longs to serve the beloved on bended knee. We see this in the example of Christ for His bride, for He literally served His bride the Church on bended knee when He knelt before the disciples to wash their feet. It was as He said: the Son of Man came not to be served, but to serve, and to give His life. The true man feels the same: he longs to serve his bride, and to give up his life for her. The feeling, tragically, may pass (the divorce rate in North America now runs at about 50%), but the failure to keep promises does not mean the promises were not well made. When one is in love, one taps into the secret rhythm of the universe, and finds the true nature of love revealed.

I suggest therefore the husband's headship of the wife is not simply a matter of the man winning the power struggle between man and woman. In much of feminism, the war (or at least the competition) between the sexes is the defining element in their inter-relationship, and when seen through this prism, of course male headship is seen askew, as the man winning at the woman's expense. In this battle, one must win, and one must lose. But true love transcends the struggle between the sexes, as each person seeks to serve the other. The common aim is not to win, but to serve. Thus children do not see Mommy and Daddy as competitors, but as both having their own and differing gifts to contribute to the common family. Fairy-tales witness to how these differences open possibilities for the man's gallant service to the woman, and when men are in love, they discover the fairy-tales speak the truth. Headship, if it is Christian, translates into loving service. That is perhaps why most of the great love poetry in the world has been written by Christians. This model of headship/subordination should be compatible with a feminism that values women, since the husbandly head places the same value on his wife as he does on himself. As St Paul said, "Husbands should love their wives as their own bodies" (Eph 5.28).

Feminism and Power in the Church

It is just here, I suggest, at the cross-roads and choice between love and power, that feminism loses its way. Perhaps no word or concept is dearer to the feminist heart than "empowerment." Feminism, in all its forms, both the praiseworthy and the less so, may be seen as the quest for power. In some instances, this quest for power is justified (one thinks of wives suffering domestic violence who strive to achieve power for the sake of their emotional health and physical safety). But when power becomes the dominant and unitive component in one's life, it does so at the cost of its Christian component. Christ crucified, as well as His martyrs after Him, reveal that the dominant and unitive element of our lives must be love, not power, for truth is revealed ultimately in love. Human power is utterly incapable of promoting the quest for authentic and true life, and of transforming and healing the heart. No one was more powerless than Christ was on the cross, and no demonstration of love was more potent, yet it was this powerlessness and love which saved the world. Christian feminism draws its inspiration primarily from a secular model, one in which power is the fundamental goal (as it was, quite properly, in the American Civil Rights movement). Such an inspiration and model utterly fails, however, as a Christian way forward toward authenticity and transformation, and a theology based on the quest for power will bear no lasting spiritual fruit. Secular feminism speaks of rights, empowerment, is frequently angry, and glories in strength. The Christian way speaks of gifts, not rights, of love, not power. It knows that "human anger does not accomplish the righteousness of God" (Jas 1.20). It knows that our only glory is in the cross, in the acceptance of our own powerlessness, which itself makes way for the transcendent power of God (2 Cor 12.8–10).

The demand that the priesthood be open to women is frequently presented as the quest for justice, for redress of inequities, for women's empowerment. Priesthood is often seen as a locus of human power (which all too often it has become), and women want a share in that power.[36] This concern for power (which is often, it seems, an obsession with power), is consistent with the secular model we have been considering. But in seeing the goal of priesthood as a sharing of power, feminists misunderstand the nature of priesthood.[37] Priesthood properly understood is not about power. A priesthood which truly conforms to the gospel views the clerical office as an opportunity for service, to wash the feet of the laity and the

---

[36]This is reflected in the fact that photos of women clergy usually show them in clerical garb, often in contrast to male clergy who avoid such a visual assertion of clerical power.

[37]Sadly, there are many men who share that misunderstanding—too many of them clergy themselves.

world, to see that the gifts of the laity are fully utilized. That is, the priest-hood must forever cease strutting, and valuing privilege, and delighting in having their hands kissed, and respectful greetings in the market-place, and places of honor at feasts (see Lk 20.46–47). Such things are not wrong in themselves, but a priesthood that delights in them, that insists upon them and sees itself as entitled to them has lost its way. Priesthood is not about power and privilege, but about love, and thus the proper place for priests, as for any Christian, is upon the cross. Feminists who stridently demand inclusion in the priesthood seem often motivated for the desire to exercise such power themselves, and to advance their own empowerment. The Church would be better served if they protested not their own exclusion from the priesthood, but the present and lamentable ill-health of the priesthood itself. I believe that much of the Church's lack of credibility in the world, as well as the division between parish clergy and laity, is found in this distortion in the understanding of priesthood. The parish priest is all too often caught up in a power struggle with his parish (or a quieter power struggle with his bishop). The answer is not for the priest to have enough power to win the struggle, but to see that the struggle only exists because the priesthood is conceived in terms of power. Here, I submit, is a church reform worth working toward.

This is, I believe, the true significance of the example provided by the Theotokos. The fact that she never functioned as a priest is sometimes cited by opponents of the ordination of women. The classic statement of the argument is provided by St Epiphanius (d. 403), who wrote about the possibility of women priests (that is, the *im*possibility of women priests) in his condemnation of the heretical groups which allowed it. In his *Panarion* (ch. 79), he writes,

> "Never at any time has a woman been a priest. . . . If it were ordained by God that women should be priests or have any canonical function in the Church, Mary herself, if anyone, should have functioned as priest in the New Testament. She was counted worthy to bear the king of all in her own womb, the heavenly God, the Son of God. Her womb became a temple, and by God's kindness and an awesome mystery was prepared to be the dwelling place of the Lord's human nature. But it

was not God's pleasure. She was not even entrusted with the administration of baptism—for Christ could have been baptized by her rather
than by John."

The argument is easier to disdain than to refute. The bishop of Cyprus
argues that Mary's supreme holiness, the worthiness which fitted her to be
the living temple of the divine King, would have qualified her for office in
the Church, if such a thing were possible. The fact that she held no office in
the apostolic Church reveals that the disqualifying factor was to be found
solely in her gender. This is true, but I believe there is a deeper significance
in the fact that the Mother of God did not hold clerical rank—namely that
ecclesiastical office is irrelevant to the quest for true holiness. The combination of supreme sanctity and the absence of "any canonical function in
the Church" (to quote St Epiphanius) shows us that status before God has
nothing to do with ordination.

More than that, the honor that comes with ecclesiastical rank can actually be an *impediment* to growth in holiness, so that holiness is most easily
attained when one renounces the entitlement to honor which all too often
comes with ordination. A certain spiritual *kenosis* is required of any who
would progress in sanctity. This *kenosis*, I believe, is illustrated in the life
of the Theotokos, who did not put herself forward to be honored in the
Church and did not seek ecclesiastical office. Indeed, in the list of people
in the Jerusalem church mentioned by Luke in Acts 1.13–14, Mary the
mother of Jesus does not even come at the head of the list, but in the
middle. It is almost as if she were trying to disappear into the crowd of
the faithful there, not putting herself forward as the Mother of the Lord
or insisting upon the pre-eminence which was her "right." She seems to
have preferred a place far from the lime-light which inevitably comes with
authority. Similarly she is absent from much of the Gospel record (a fact
often brought to our attention by Protestants in polemical debate)—not
because she had no pre-eminence, but because she delighted to remain in
the background, vanishing (as it were) into her Son and into His body the
church. In all her earthly life, she emptied herself, not seeking authority
or honor. As the embodiment of her Son's teaching, she humbled herself,
leaving any future exaltation in the hands of God.

In this she left a lesson for all in the church, men as well as women, which is that exaltation and blessing and holiness come only through humility and self-emptying. If one has the task (one is sometimes tempted to add "the misfortune") to assume Holy Orders, one must be all the more careful to embrace the way of *kenosis* and humility. The path of true priesthood is the path of humility, of service, of foot-washing. Prideful insistence upon one's perceived rights betrays this calling. She who is now "more honorable than the cherubim and more glorious beyond compare than the seraphim" calls us to the kenotic humility of her Son.

Women in Secular Authority

Though, as we have attempted to show, male headship in family and church is an abiding principle for the Christian, women have exercised positions of leadership in the secular world (one thinks of the empress in Byzantine times[38])—a leadership which was never questioned by the bishops and which was always accepted by the Church at large. It will not do to side with John Knox, who, in his tract *Against the Monstrous Regiment of Women*, simply dismissed it out of hand as unnatural and unbiblical. Clearly women in the ancient world as well as in our own make completely satisfactory empresses, queens, presidents and prime ministers. The question is asked, "If a woman can govern a country, why not a church?"

The question is an excellent one, because it brings us to the heart of the issue, which is the difference between a family and a government. Briefly put, a family is a divine institution, created by God for the creation and formation of human beings, whereas a government is a human institution, created by men for the preservation of order and the restraint of chaos and evil. Thus families have more to do with our basic humanity and those roles than does a government.

[38] We note, however, that even in Byzantium there was not total parity between male and female rulers. The Empress Irene (d. 803) was the first woman to reign in her own right, but the official state documents still referred to her as a masculine *basileus*, not a feminine *basilissa*, thus giving official lip service to male leadership as normative. See Tamara Talbot Rice, *Everyday Life in Byzantium* (New York, NY: Barnes and Noble, 1967), 38.

Governments are human creations, as is governmental authority. In this sense, the governmental authority of one human being over another is something like the authority of the master over the slave—not in the sense that rulers are despots, but rather in the restricted sense that in Paradise there existed neither slavery nor government. It has been said that God did not make slaves, but rather that men made slaves. In the same way, I would suggest that men made government, for government did not exist in Eden. Government is the authority of a single person over a multitude of others, and in an unfallen world no government would be necessary, for its people would live in love and care for one another without laws or compulsion. St Paul admits as much when he said that rulers "were not a cause of fear for good behavior, but for evil," and that consequently the ruler "did not bear the sword in vain, for he is a minister of God, an avenger who brings wrath on the one who practices evil" (Rom 13.3–4). Had we never left the Garden, there would be no cause for anyone to "bear the sword." In the apostle's view, "authority is established by God" (Rom 13.1) principally for the restraint of evil. Just as the Law would be unnecessary in an unfallen world (for "the Law was not made for the righteous, but for those who are lawless and rebellious, for the ungodly and sinners"; 1 Tim 1.9), so the authority of rulers would be unnecessary. Given the fallenness of the world, God allowed some people to govern others—and even blessed such an arrangement among His chosen people.[39] But this divine blessing on government does not mean that it would have existed in an unfallen world.

The family is a divine creation, and it existed in Eden prior to the Fall.[40] As such, it exists on a different plane from such things as governments, and it creates and revolves around realities more fundamental to human nature. Governments create things such as taxation, the armed service of soldiers willing to die, and the civil service of people working to keep the complex machinery of civilization running. In democracies, we create systems of voting, and ways of distributing political power. In a liberal

[39] Though even here we note that His original intention involved the authority of tribes (i.e., families), and that His blessing of kingship came as a somewhat reluctant concession—see 1 Sam 8.

[40] The truth of this, I suggest, does not depend upon a certain view of the historicity of Genesis' early chapters.

democratic government we find the assertion, for example, that "all men [*sic*] are created equal." That is, for the purposes of running a democracy, of enfranchising its citizens with the vote and distributing power, we act as if each of its citizens were the equal of the other, and as if each person were the same and interchangeable. For political and governmental purposes, they *are* interchangeable and equal. But of course that is a fiction. People are not equal—some are smarter than others, some more talented, some more industrious, some more valuable to the working of society. But for purposes of government, democracy adopts the legal fiction that all are interchangeable, since their votes are interchangeable. There is nothing in the least wrong with this. Because government is something created by man, we can quite legitimately change the system of government if we think we can improve on it or find a better one.

But families do not have the same liberty. Since the family was created by God, we are not free to tinker with it and re-arrange it at will, as we are with governments. We cannot restructure the family so that the woman takes the role of father, or the man takes the role of mother, or the grand-daughter takes the role of grandfather, for these roles have their roots in gender and age. We cannot rearrange the basic structure so that a man has ten wives, or so that he can trade in his wife for a younger replacement every few years. Admittedly, both polygamy and divorce were allowed Israel "for their hardness of heart," but the Lord has taught us that "from the beginning it has not been this way" (Mt 19.8). God's original blue-print for the family was for one man and one woman to become one flesh and to stay that way for the procreation of children. The entire interactions of mother-father-children-grandparents (if any) are arranged so that they all contribute to making of a matrix wherein children can grow as they should. As C.S. Lewis said about these family interactions, "If you subtract any member, you have not simply reduced the family in number, you have inflicted an injury on its structure. Its unity is a unity of unlikes, almost of incommensurables."[41] It is only as we conform to this pattern that we can attain the spiritual, psychological and emotional health intended by God. This is not to deny that people can survive and even thrive when

[41]C.S. Lewis, "Membership," in Walter Hooper, ed., *Fern-seed and Elephants* (London: Harper Collins, 1975), 16.

the wholeness and health of a family is broken. The human heart is very resilient, and people can cope with and heal from all sorts of things. But the original intention of God for the family remains, even if we sometimes deviate from it.

It is because of this fundamental ontological inequality and essential dissimilarity of government with family that women can successfully be the head of such artificial creations as the State, but not be the head of a divine creation such as the family.[42] A woman can rule the land as a queen or president, for this authority, though powerful and palpable, is artificial. Her role as ruler in the state is not fundamental to her gender, as her role as mother would be in the family. Gender, as well as age, do not define and inform the role of ruler as they do the roles of father, mother, children and grandparent. Government involves the outer edges of our lives; family forms us at our center. A subject may have loyalty toward his queen, but that love and loyalty will still be of a different nature and not be as deep as his love for his mother—or if it is, most would not commend the subject for patriotic loyalty, but fault him for a deficit of filial love. This shows that family is more fundamental than the state, for the family creates the matrix in which children grow to health and know who they are. The role of the family is basic to our identity in a way that the role of state could never be. When functioning in a family, we are our truest selves; when functioning as citizens in the State, we are fulfilling a duty.

It is for this reason that the queen (or Madame President) would properly lay aside the robes of state (metaphorically speaking) when she closed the public doors and reclined with her husband. She would exercise royal or presidential authority when she governed her subjects, ruled their bodies, and promoted the good of society. But there would be something wrong if she took her public authority into the private chambers with her husband, and demanded from him in their private and intimate life the same subordination demanded of her subjects and citizens in the public square. She ought not to think that being ruler meant that she was the head of her husband in their private life, and that all the apostolic pre-

---

[42]Obviously women heading single parent families after divorce or the death of the spouse will do their best, and can rely on God's grace and help. I am speaking of the intended ideal.

cepts about husband and wife were overturned because she possessed secular authority to rule. As a good ruler, she would discern the separate spheres in which God called her to move, and would not import authority from one into the other. Thus, a queen might rule something as light and transitory as the world. She might not rule something as primordial and weighty as the family. When she danced with her husband, she would let him lead.

This difference between government and family holds for the Church family as well. The roles and realities in the Church involve its members in their most basic selves, as even do the roles of the family. That is why St Paul calls the Church "the household of God" (Greek=*oikos theou*) in 1 Timothy 3.14. Women may possess and wield secular authority, because such authority is not rooted in our most basic selves, and has nothing to do with gender. Authority in the Church, which involves spiritual fatherhood, does access the power and reality of gender. Their right to secular power does not translate into a right to ordination.

Women as Evangelists, Prophets, and Teachers

In considering the topic of the ordination of women, we have suggested that women may not exercise personal spiritual authority in the Church in the same way as male presbyters do, because spiritual authority is rooted in fatherhood. But what of the New Testament figures of Junia (Rom 16.7), of Prisca (Rom 16.3), and of Philip the evangelist's daughters, who prophesied (Acts 21.9)? These women spoke and taught, and were praised by St Paul—the same one who insisted women could not be teachers. We also read of women advising other women, as "teachers of good" (Titus 2.4). These were all women with legitimate ministries in the Church. While a full exegesis of these passages is beyond the scope of the present work, we will consider them briefly in turn. We will see that their teaching roles were very different from that of the "shepherds and teachers" to whom Paul referred in Ephesians 4.11, so that the existence of these women teachers does not contradict the apostolic ban on women as official *didaskaloi* in the church.

JUNIA

Junia, whose name is paired with Andronicus in Romans 16.7, is some-times regarded as a man, with the name "Junias." In this passage at the end of his letter to the Romans, Paul bids his readers, "Greet Androni-cus and Junia/s (Greek=*Iounian*), my kinsmen and my fellow-prisoners, who are notable among the apostles." The word *Iounian* is in the accusa-tive, and so grammatically might be derived from either as a man's name, Junias,[43] or a woman's name, Junia. Since it seems likely that Andronicus is here paired with his spouse (as was Aquila with Prisca earlier in the passage), and since the feminine "Junia" is well-attested with over 250 Roman inscriptions alone, while the masculine "Junias" is entirely unat-tested in any evidence,[44] I take the name to be that of a woman, Junia. She is described, with Andronicus (presumably her husband), as "notable among the apostles," which might mean that the apostles thought them notable, or that they were notable apostles. I take the latter meaning to be correct—as did St John Chrysostom. In his sermon on this passage (*Hom-ily on Romans*, ch. 31), he says, "These two were of note because of their works and achievements. Think how great the devotion of this woman Junia must have been, that she should be worthy to be called an apostle!"

Chrysostom's comment reveals how he regarded the nature of her apostleship—that it was an honorary title, bestowed to honor her for her devotion and works. Andronicus is described as an apostle. Since he was described as being Paul's "kinsman" (i.e., Jewish), and as being "in Christ before" Paul (i.e., he converted to Christ before Paul did), it is possible he was one of the Seventy Christ sent out in Palestine, recorded in Luke 10.1. It also possible that Paul here uses the term "apostle" more loosely, as he does when describing Epaphroditus in Philippians 2.25. Either way, his wife Junia shared the title and the honor, since she shared her husband's ministry by supporting him in it, possibly mixing with and speaking to the women they encountered in their travels. We note that Junia's minis-try is tied to that of her husband's, and that (as Chrysostom suggests) the

---

[43]The RSV opts for the masculine "Junias," and renders the last part of the verse, "they are *men* of note among the apostles" (emphasis mine).

[44]Lynn Cohick, *Women in the World of the Earliest Christians* (Grand Rapids, MI: Baker Academic, 2009), 214.

description of her as an apostle is an honorific.[45] The example of Junia therefore does not represent an exception to the Pauline ban on women exercising authoritative church office. Junia's ministry was much like that of Prisca's, considered next.

PRISCA

Prisca ("Priscilla" to her friends, the diminutive of Prisca) worked with her husband Aquila. They had a church in their house (1 Cor 16.19), and it is reasonable to suppose that they exercised a teaching ministry together there of some sort. They together instructed Apollos regarding the deficiencies of his faith (notably his need for Christian baptism, supplementing his prior Johannine baptism; Acts 18.26). Since the text says, "they took him" (Greek=*proselabonto auton*), we may conclude that such instruction was given discretely and privately, in contrast to Apollos' public and bold proclamation of Jesus, doubtless to spare him embarrassment. Prisca is always found paired with her husband in the NT references. Given that usually and in defiance of custom her name precedes that of her husband's (e.g., Acts 18.18, 26; Rom 16.3; 2 Tim 4.19, though not in 1 Cor 16.19), it is reasonable to conclude that she was the more dominant of the two, perhaps through having inherited a greater social standing. It is significant that hers was a team ministry exercised with her husband, and that she did not function apart from him. Nonetheless, she did exercise a ministry of catechesis. Since Paul severely censures women who aspire to public teaching in the church (e.g., 1 Cor 14.33–36), and since he has no word of censure for Prisca, it is likely that her teaching was given privately, along with her husband—which is the pattern presented in Acts 18.26. This text also shows that their main task was that of missionaries.[46]

---

[45]Compare the practice of describing rich women benefactors as *archisynagōgus*, despite the women not actually exercising that function. See C.C. Ryrie, *The Role of Women in the Church* (Chicago: Moody Press, 1970), 88: "although honorary titles of the synagogue were conferred on women for outstanding service (usually charity), these titles had no official significance"—i.e., they did not actually rule as the men did.

[46]Ammonius in his commentary says, "We must believe that women passed on the Faith: see how completely desirous of salvation Apollos was . . . he did not consider it worthless to learn the fullness of the Faith from a woman." *Catena on the Acts of the Apostles* at Acts 18.26, quoted in Francis Martin and Evan Smith, *Acts*, Ancient Christian Commentary on Scripture NT 5 (Downers Grove, IL: InterVarsity Press, 2006), 231.

Junia and Prisca shared some characteristics. First of all, their ministries were tied to those of their husbands, so that they are examples not so much of women apostles or teachers as the feminine parts of husband-and-wife team ministries. Also, their teaching ministry was a part of their larger peripatetic apostolic ministry—their primary task was not that of a settled teacher in the local church who exercised authority in that community, but that of an itinerant missionary.[47] They shared the gospel of Christ with those who had never yet heard it, leading them to faith and baptism—and then moved on. They were to have successors in the coming centuries—one thinks of St Nina, enlightener of Georgia. As evangelists, their role was different from those authoritative settled teachers of the local church communities. What mattered in the case of the missionaries was not any personal authority as exercised in the matrix of community, but the kerygmatic message. Anyone, man or woman or child, could preach the gospel, for no personal authority was needed, and no institutional authority was involved. Their words were not given within the context of a community which looked to them to rule them. Their words led their hearers to faith, and then the preachers left the newly formed Christian community in the care of others. Doubtless they would continue to enjoy a moral authority with their new converts, but there was no opportunity for the exercise of an institutional authority. The gospel proclamations of Junia, Prisca, and later, Nina, were of this type. Thus, the examples of these women do not contradict the New Testament teaching barring women from the offices of *didaskalos*, or presbyter-bishop, for this latter office involved personal authority in the settled community in a way that the ministry of missionary did not.

PROPHETS: THE DAUGHTERS OF PHILIP WHO PROPHESIED

In this sense, the itinerant ministries of missionaries preaching the gospel had much in common with the exercise of prophecy, for the authority lay in the message, not the medium, in the preaching, not the preacher. And so we must examine the role of prophets in the Church.[48] St Paul seems

[47] A role shared by St Mary Magdalene, "apostle to the apostles."
[48] An example of such prophecy may be found in Agabus (Acts 21.11). Prophets received a message from God and transmitted the oracle, in the tradition of the Old Testament prophets. The formula "thus says the Holy Spirit" (Greek=*tade legei to pneuma to agion*)

to have accepted without difficulty the situation of women prophesying in the local *synaxis*; he only commands that they cover their heads while doing so (1 Cor 11.5). Further, he says that "you can all prophesy one by one" (1 Cor 14.31), and there is no suggestion that such utterances were confined to the men. Also, Philip the evangelist's daughters "who prophesied" (Greek=*prophēteuousai*) are mentioned by Luke in Acts 21.9 with no suggestion that female prophets were unusual or were not allowed. Indeed, the ancient prophecy of Joel 2.28, cited by Peter in his Pentecostal sermon in Acts 2.17, explicitly says that "your sons *and your daughters* shall prophesy," and this prophecy evidently found abundant fulfillment in the apostolic Church of the first century. Women could bring forth a word of prophecy just as men could, and there were doubtless women prophets in the Pauline churches.

But bringing forth a prophetic word, while doubtless bestowing a social dignity on the prophet, did not involve the exercise of abiding personal authority or the expectation that a prophet would rule the Church as the presbyters did. It is the prophetic *word* which had authority; the prophet proclaiming it was simply the messenger, the conduit through which the message came. Authority resided in the message itself, not the messenger.[49] Confirmation of the lack of abiding personal authority on the part of prophets is found in 1 Corinthians 14.29–30. The prophets speak, but it is "the others" (Greek=*oi alloi*)—almost certainly the presbyters, but anyway someone "other" than the prophets—who sit in judgment on the prophetic utterance and discern (Greek=*diakrinō*) its validity.[50]

echoes the Old Testament "thus says the Lord," *tade legei kyrios* (e.g., Jer 22.1 LXX). To this NT example we may also add the OT example of Deborah, from Judg 4–5. She "judged" Israel, in that she was instrumental in their shaking off the Gentile yoke of Sisera and his armies, but she is described as a "prophetess" in Judg 4.4, and that is her primary role.

[49]The social prestige of the prophets allowed them to give thanks according to their prophetic gifts at the agape, exempting them from the obligation to use set forms, but this privilege is far removed from the ruling authority of the presbyterate. See the *Didache*, ch. 11: "Let the prophets give thanks however they wish." I take it that the meal for which they gave thanks was the agape, not the Eucharist. This was also the view of Gregory Dix, *The Shape of the Liturgy* (London: Dacre Press, 1945), 91.

[50]It is grammatically possible that "the others" refers to the other prophets, but I think this unlikely, since Paul's concern is to provide a balance to the prophets. If Paul had meant to forego this balance, one would expect him to write about "the other prophets," not simply "the others."

And "if a revelation is made" to the one "who is seated" in judgment, so that the proffered prophecy is not received, "let the first keep silent"—i.e., let the prophet accept the negative verdict of those sitting by in judgment. Clearly, institutional authority lay with someone other than the prophets, at least so far as the prophecy itself was concerned. Thus, women prophets along with men prophets, bore no personal authority in the *synaxis*. That authority was possessed by "the others." With prophets, as with itinerant apostles or missionaries, their ministry consisted mainly in bringing forth the Word, either the saving *kerygma* (in the case of missionaries) or an edifying message (in the case of prophets). This ministry bestowed dignity and honor upon those who were called to it, but it did not entail the exercise of abiding pastoral authority. That is why it could be fulfilled by women as well as men.

WOMEN TEACHERS OF GOOD

In Titus 2.3–4, we read that older women are "to be reverent in their behavior, not malicious gossips, nor enslaved to much wine," but to be "teachers of good,[51] that they may advise[52] the young women to love their husbands,[53] to love their children, to be sensible, pure, workers at home,[54] being subject to their own husbands." Here we find older women exercising an informal ministry of teaching, not simply by example, but also by precept, as the Christians of various ages and different families mixed together socially. Though the author of the epistle does not elaborate on the state of these women *kalodidaskaloi*, I suggest that the exhortation presupposes that the women in question possessed at least some wealth and rank. Certainly the culture of the time would have made it difficult for slave women or women of lower social standing to teach and advise their social superiors. This teaching was thus of an informal kind, and required no official church rank for its performance. It was the sort of teaching and

[51]Greek=*kalodidaskalous*.
[52]Greek=*sōphronizōsin*, sometimes used with the meaning, "to call one to one's senses."
[53]Greek=*philandrous einai*.
[54]Greek=*oikourgous*.

moral exhortation that would flow naturally from educated women in that social situation.

A later and famous example of such a teacher of good was Macrina, sister of Gregory of Nyssa, who indeed called her his "teacher." She was a woman of rank and wealth, who used her resources to establish the Church and promote piety. Her teaching was given as part of her interaction with the world. In that day, wealthy women were expected to have learning (Plutarch says that a good wife should be educated and know philosophy[55]), and those for whom they acted as patrons doubtless would benefit from their philosophical learning in the course of their social interaction. Macrina was one of these women, whose piety found its voice in discoursing to those around her. We note that this teaching drew its authority from the wealth and dignity of the women giving it, not from their official rank in the Church.

What then is the difference between the two types of teaching? The difference is rooted in the distinction between ordained ministry and unordained ministry. Ordained teachers, the official *didaskaloi* of the Church (paired with shepherds in Eph 4.11[56]), speak with an authority which is personal and official. As those officially representing the Church to world, they bear a higher degree of accountability and responsibility. They are called to "rightly define the word of God's truth,"[57] and thus, their teaching comes under more intense scrutiny, since it forms the basis for the Eucharistic fellowship of the gathered Church. That is, if their teaching is orthodox, the faithful gather around the teacher as he presides at the Eucharist, so that his teaching forms the basis of ecclesial unity, whereas if the teaching is deemed heretical, the faithful would gather around his orthodox rival. That is why the ordained teacher is more subject to scrutiny and canonical censure. The more informal and private teaching of the unordained people such as Macrina did not form the sacramental basis for the Eucharistic gathering. They had no personal authority as did

[55]Cited in Lynn H. Cohick's *Women in the World of the Earliest Christians* (Grand Rapids, MI: Baker Academic, 2009), 71.

[56]The words "shepherds" and "teachers" are both governed by the same words "and some" (Greek=*tous de*).

[57]The phrase, originally from 2 Tim 2.15, is applied to the role of the bishop in the Anaphora in the Liturgy.

the ordained, and so were less subject to canonical censure. The informal work of women *kalodidaskaloi* was utterly different than that of the formal *didaskalos* and the clergy.

It is important to take care that we do not devalue this informal work of teaching, which was never accompanied by any formal ecclesiastical authority. Christian women, of all social ranks, have always taught their daughters and granddaughters as well as their sons and grandsons, passing on the Faith through precept as well as by example. Official authority, ordination, and title were never required nor desired for this worthy and essential work of teaching. An unhealthy clericalism would devalue all work that is not done by clergy, and deny the full dignity of these *kalodidaskaloi*. Such devaluation would be unfortunate. The Faith has been passed down through the generations in large measure through the ministries of such women. They do not require ordination, but recognition. They do not need to be "empowered," since they already possess all the power they need to fulfill the ministry to which God calls them. Rather, they need to be celebrated and acknowledged.

Feminine Roles in the Church

If women may not function as office-bearers such as bishops or priests in the Church, one may ask, what is their role? We begin by observing that the question is a modern one, and reflects modern concerns (not to say modern obsessions). Earlier ages were not so concerned with gender issues as we are, but with non-gender-specific themes such as holiness. They did not ask the question, "What roles may women as women play in the Church?," but rather "How may women (and men) become holy?"[58] This latter question more accurately reflects the thought-world and concerns of the Scriptures and the Fathers than does the former question. But each age asks its own questions, and deserves answers, even if these questions spring from a world-view different from that of the Fathers. Accordingly, we offer some response.

[58]I suspect that they would have applauded Fr Thomas Hopko's statement, "Persons, not natures or genders, have callings from God." See his article, "Presbyter/Bishop: A Masculine Ministry," in Thomas Hopko, ed., *Women and the Priesthood* (Crestwood, NY: St Vladimir's Seminary Press, 1999), 162.

In dealing with this question, it is important also to observe first that here we move from the sure foundations of Scripture and the Fathers into the more debatable realm of theological speculation. That is, the Scriptural writers and the Fathers after them dealt explicitly with the question, "May women be ordained to authoritative church office such as presbyters?" and they answered the question in the negative. (We moderns may reject their answer for one reason for another, but it seems clear enough that this was in fact their answer.) The modern question, "What are the specific charisms and roles of women?" was never explicitly raised by the Scriptural writers or the Fathers. Our answers therefore must be more tentative. In short, we were on firm ground in answering the first question. We are extrapolating and surmising in attempting an answer to the second.

THE CHURCH'S MATERNAL ROLE

In elaborating the role of the feminine in the Church, we may return to the insights of Brook Herbert, cited above. In her essay titled, "Towards a Recovery of the Theology of Patriarchy," she distinguishes between the roles of father and mother within the family, characterizing the father's role as one of protection, individuation, and legitimization. What then of the mother's role within the family? Herbert writes, "The feminine predisposition towards intuitive knowledge is . . . closely allied to the woman's creational predisposition for motherhood. Physically, she is constituted to carry a life within her . . . The intuitive principle within the female psyche allows the mother to live and move in harmony with the rhythm of the new life within her and later to nurture the growing life of the child. Perceptually, she is attuned to the mystery of creation."[59] I would sum up these roles as birth-giving, nurturing, and beautifying.

We have seen how the father's roles in the family are fulfilled in the church community by the priest/bishop. How are these three roles of birth-giving, nurturing, and beautifying fulfilled in the church community? I would suggest that they are fulfilled by the community as a whole—it is the Church *as Church* which gives birth to new members, which nurtures the young Christians in its midst, which produces beauty to enrich the

---

[59]Herbert, op. cit., 296.

lives of her children. That is why the church community has traditionally been experienced as "Mother Church." The male priest is not "balanced" in the Church by an individual female presence, such as the priest's wife or office-bearing women. The *entire church community* fulfills these maternal roles, both by exemplifying a community of nurture, healing, love, and beauty, and also by the exercise of the ministries of individual Christians of both genders within the community. The paternal role of the pastor is thus balanced communally by the maternal role of the entire community. (It is in this sense that church custom speaks of the bishop being "married" to his diocese, so that the diocese is described as having been "widowed" when the bishop dies. The complementarity of bishop with his diocese reflects the balance of any pastor with his community.)

Let us examine these "maternal" roles one by one. The function of birth-giving—i.e., of converting and baptizing—is not done by women alone. Men as well as women are called to be evangelists, to reach out with the gospel (we think again of the husband-wife team of Prisca and Aquila, and of Andronicus and Junia). Also, both men and women share the gospel informally with their friends (what Michael Green described as "gossiping the gospel"[60]). Many people who convert to the Christian Faith do so because of the witness of and inter-action with an entire church community. As the Lord Himself said, "By this all will know you are My disciples, if you have love for one another" (Jn 13.35). A spiritually healthy community will grow and produce converts. Further, this spiritual health of the local church community is not irrelevant when it comes to the children who were baptized as infants coming to intentional faith as they grow up. It takes a village to raise a child, it is said, and similarly it takes a parish to raise a child as a devout Christian. The faith, teaching, and example of the child's parents may be paramount in the child coming to mature faith, but this does not devalue the role played by the parish as a whole in this process. This role of spiritual birth-giving, therefore, is not and cannot be confined to women, or to certain individuals of either gender. It is a function of the entire local church, though of course individuals with a ministry of evangelism will make their own contribution.

[60]Michael Green, *Evangelism in the Early Church* (London: Hodder and Stoughton, 1970), 173.

It is the same with the function of nurturing young Christians, either those born to Christians and growing up in the church, or those newly converted to Christ at a more mature age. The maternal role of nourishment and nurture, of healing and encouraging growth, is fulfilled by the church community as a whole and by certain ministries within it. Once again we recognize how crucial is a church's spiritual health—a healthy church community will produce healthy Christians, and a dysfunctional, unloving, angry community will produce Christians who are to one degree or another spiritually sick. (The same is true of families.) A community in which its members affirm and love one another, offering praise and forgiveness according to need, and welcome the use of others' spiritual gifts, will nurture and help its members to grow up in spiritual health. This nurturing role is fulfilled also by those with special ministries and with the spiritual gifts enabling them to fulfill those ministries. Here we are thinking of ministries of prophecy, healing, and counseling, ministries which women as well as men may fulfill. These ministries do not require "official" status or ordination.[61] They can be and are exercised by laity within the community (though, of course, ordained clergy might have such spiritual gifts and roles as well). The ministries are not gender-specific, but together fulfill the maternal role of nurturing.

It is the same for the function of producing beauty which enriches the lives of those growing within the community of faith. Such beautifying ministries are those of producing music, architecture, vestments, incense, church furnishing, and iconography—all those things which together make the church temple and church experience one of beauty that can feed the soul. All of these ministries and tasks can be fulfilled by men as well as women, and they do not require ordination.

This truth—that individuals of both genders work together to fulfill a corporate role which is essentially maternal—bears witness to another truth, and one which is at the root of it. Namely, the Church is essentially feminine. It is the bride of Christ, at the same time both virgin and mother.

[61]Compare *Apostolic Tradition*, ch. 10, on "widows": "Let the widow be installed with the word only . . . but a hand shall not be laid on her, because she does not lift up the sacrifice, nor does she a have a proper liturgy. For the laying on of hands is with the clergy, on account of the liturgy." Alistair Stewart-Sykes, tr., *Hippolytus: On the Apostolic Tradition*, Popular Patristics Series no. 22 (Crestwood, NY: St Vladimir's Seminary Press, 2001), 95.

As C.S. Lewis once observed of the members of Christ's Church, "We are all feminine to Him."[62] That is, men equally with women are typologically feminine, being part of the bride of Christ, and having the Son of God as their heavenly bridegroom. The work of both genders in the Church therefore fulfills the role of the work of "Mother Church." The community in its totality, and also the work of individual and non-gender-specific ministries such as evangelist, prophet, healer, iconographer, fulfill the role of mother for the children of the Church.

This means, of course, that the ministry of presbyter or pastor, of the parish priest, is of a fundamentally different type from other ministries in the Church. As intimated above, other ministries such as evangelist, prophet, healer, counselor, or the multitude of other gifted roles in the church community, function on a different track from that of the priest. This latter role is determinative of the ecclesial reality of the community—the people gather around the priest and are a church because of his ministry. As the authoritative definer of the Faith and thus the celebrant of the Eucharist, his ministry lays the foundation for everything else. In this sense his ministry prepares the way for other ministries and gifted roles and allows them to exist. That is why ordination (and with it, public ecclesial accountability) is required for this role more than for (say) the ministry of healer. In the words of the *Apostolic Tradition* quoted above, "the laying on of hands is with the clergy, on account of the liturgy." Ordination is required for this service of the altar (served in varying ways by deacons, presbyters, and bishops), because the Eucharist of the altar creates the Church and lays the foundation for everything else—including the existence of other ministries not requiring a like ordination.

FEMALE CHARISMS AND SPIRITUALITY AS FEMININE

A number of theologians have written about female charisms in the Church, and root these in the feminine nature of women. In this reading, the masculine nature is reflected in the Logos, the Son of God, while the feminine is reflected in the Holy Spirit,[63] who is referred to in feminine

[62]Lewis, *Priestesses in the Church*, op. cit., p 239.
[63]For example, Evdokimov, in his book, *The Sacrament of Love* (Crestwood, NY: St Vladimir's Seminary Press, 1985), 37, citing the *Didascalia*, speaks of the deacon holding

terms.[64] The feminine therefore has a special connection with the Holy Spirit and in some sense is the human reflection of the Spirit. Indeed, this understanding posits spirituality as distinctly feminine. Evdokimov describes woman as "the spiritual instrument of human nature"[65] so that "the religious principle of dependence, of receptivity, of communion, is expressed more directly through woman . . . it is the feminine soul that is the least removed from the source, creation. *The Bible exalts woman as the instrument of spiritual receptivity in human nature.*"[66] Thus the connection of the feminine with the Holy Spirit is assured: "In his spiritual being, man is ontologically joined to Christ; the woman is ontologically linked to the Holy Spirit."[67] Indeed, she is "linked in her very essence to the Holy Spirit."[68]

Not surprisingly then, writers like Evdokimov contend for a privileged place for femininity in the economy of salvation. Indeed, he all but identifies femininity with holiness, to the point of demonizing the masculine. He writes:

> Though he may be conqueror, adventurer, builder, a man is not paternal in his essence . . . there is nothing immediate in a man's nature that corresponds directly to the religious category of fatherhood . . . it is the feminine soul that is closest to the sources of creation. . . . The more civilization becomes secularized, the more masculine it is, the more desperate it becomes. . . . Feminine motherhood, the religious specificity of human nature, corresponds directly to the divine fatherhood, which is a characteristic of the essence of God."[69]

---

the place of Christ and the deaconess holding the place of the Holy Spirit.

[64]Evdokimov, in his *Woman and the Salvation of the World* (220) refers with approval to the logion in the "Gospel of the Hebrews" in which Christ refers to "My mother, the Holy Spirit," and to the expression of Sergius Bulgakov describing the Spirit as "hypostatic motherhood." Bobrinskoy also says "the feminine gender of *ruah* emphasizes the interiority of the Spirit and the maternal power of the One who bestows life" (op. cit., 223).

[65]Paul Evdokimov, *The Sacrament of Love*, 34.

[66]Ibid., 35 (italics original).

[67]Ibid., 37.

[68]Evdokimov, *Woman and the Salvation of the World*, 215.

[69]Ibid., 152, 156.

Thus, "sanctity is more at home to woman" so that "Tertullian's words about 'the soul that is naturally Christian' apply above all to women."[70] Evdokimov is sure that "the doctrine of predestination could never have originated from a feminine soul."[71] This approach values women and their gifts since holiness ecclesially subsists in the feminine.

What are we to make of all this? There are a number of problems with this approach. We mention three of them.

The first problem with this approach is that the Scriptures give no encouragement to the view of the divine bifurcation regarding human gender, so that men are joined to Christ while women are linked to the Holy Spirit, and that women's charisms therefore express more fully the work of the Holy Spirit. Rather, we see both the Son and the Spirit together intimately involved in the bestowal of all spiritual gifts to both genders, and moreover that spiritual gifts are given without regard to gender.

We look first at Romans 12.4–7: "Just as we have many members in one body and all the members do not have the same function, so we, who are many, are one body in Christ, and individually members one of another. And since we have *charismata* that differ according to the grace given to us, let each exercise them accordingly: if prophecy, according to the proportion of his faith, if service, in his serving, or he who teaches, in his teaching." In this passage we see a unity of all the members of the community, a unity that transcends gender. There is no suggestion that the *charismata* are distributed with any reference to gender. Indeed, the first *charisma* mentioned, that of prophecy, we know was exercised by men and women alike, presumably in identical ways. The operative principle of distribution is referred to Christ, who gives to everyone in His body apart from considerations of gender.

This is clearer still in 1 Corinthians 12.4–13. Because of the importance of the passage, we quote it in full:

> [4]Now there are varieties of gifts, but the same Spirit. [5]And there are varieties of ministries, and the same Lord. [6]There are varieties of effects, but the same God who works all things in all. [7]But to each one

[70]Ibid., 225, 267.
[71]Ibid., 153.

is given the manifestation of the Spirit for the common good. [8]For to one is given the word of wisdom through the Spirit, and to another the word of knowledge according to the same Spirit; [9]to another faith by the same Spirit, and to another gifts of healing by the one Spirit, [10]and to another the effecting of miracles, and to another prophecy, and to another the distinguishing of spirits, to another kinds of tongues, and to another the interpretation of tongues. [11]But one and the same Spirit works all these things, distributing to each one individually just as He wills. [12]For even as the body is one and has many members, and all the members of the body, though they are many, are one body, so also is Christ. [13]For in one Spirit we were all baptized into one body, whether Jews or Greeks, whether slaves or free, and we were all made to drink of one Spirit."

We make a few observations about this passage. First, we see here all three Persons of the Trinity involved in the bestowal of all the gifts. Reference is made to "the same Spirit" giving all the *charismata*, to "the same Lord" (i.e., the Son) giving all the different variety of ministries, and to "the same God" (i.e., the Father) working all things in all recipients (v. 4–6). There is no suggestion that there is any distinction between the gifts given by the Son and those more expressive of the Spirit. Both the Son and the Spirit work with the Father in all spiritual charisms in a way which precludes any bifurcation of Son and Spirit. The role of Christ in unifying all members in one body is paired with the role of the Spirit of giving gifts to all in that body: in the body of Christ, all were baptized in the Spirit as the means of entering that body (v. 13). The unity of Son and Spirit is stressed throughout.

We also note that these gifts are given without reference to gender, with no apparent thought that some gifts are female charisms while others are male charisms. Indeed, Paul's recitation of the irrelevance of being Jew or Greek, slave or free (v. 13), reminds one of similar recitations in Colossians 3.11 ("no distinction between Greek and Jew, circumcised and uncircumcised, barbarian, Scythian, slave and free"), and the favored text Galatians 3.28 ("neither Jew nor Greek, neither slave nor free, no male and female"). The absence of one element or another in this textual triptych is not significant. That is, the absence of the reference to "barbarian" and "Scythian" in 1 Corinthians 12.13 or Galatians 3.28 does not mean that these distinctions somehow applied in Corinth or Galatia. In the same way, the absence of reference to "male and female" in 1 Corinthians 12.13 is not significant. Paul's point in all these texts is that God's salvation, saving renewal, and bestowal of gifts—in other words, His grace—is given in the Church to everyone regardless of any earthly distinction. This would mean that gender distinctions ("male and female") have no place in a Pauline understanding of spiritual charisms. Granted that Paul is not writing with the detail and rigor which would allow us to draw him easily into our modern debate, certainly these New Testament texts give no encouragement for an approach which would see this or that charism distinguished by gender, or for an ontological link of either gender to the Son or the Spirit specifically.

The second problem with this approach is the assertion of the feminine element in the Holy Spirit. Here it seems that the poetry of St Ephraim the Syrian and the Syrian tradition upon which his poetry draws is pressed into modern dogmatic service beyond what is justifiable. The history of the portrayal of the Spirit in Syriac Christianity is complicated and varied, as has been shown by Susan Ashbrook Harvey in her article "Feminine Imagery for the Divine: the Holy Spirit, the Odes of Solomon and the Early Syriac Tradition"[72] I would suggest that the references to the Spirit being feminine in that tradition should be read for their poetic power and not as theological assertions. That is, their aim is more to edify than to teach, and one should be wary of extrapolating from the poetry the dogmatic assertion that the Holy Spirit is feminine (complementing the Son as masculine). Proof that such theological gender-bending violates the intention of the original poets may be found in their poems presenting the Father and Son in terms of feminine imagery. Most famous perhaps is Ode 19 of the *Odes of Solomon*, which reads in part, "A cup of milk was offered to me and I drank it . . . the Son is the cup, and He who was milked is the Father, and she who milked Him is the Holy Spirit. Because His breasts were full and it was not necessary for His milk to be poured out without cause. The

---

[72]Found in *Saint Vladimir's Theological Quarterly*, 37.2–3 (1993), 111–139. We must not forget also to mention the work of Sebastian Brock in this field.

Holy Spirit opened her womb and mixed the milk of the two breasts of the Father and she gave the mixture to the world … "[73] The images are powerful (and more resonant in cultures which have not banished breast-feeding from public view as the West more recently has). Nonetheless the portrayal here of the Father and the Son in feminine terms does not in any way compromise their essential masculinity in theology proper,[74] nor turn the Hebrew-Christian God into a goddess, nor was that in the intention of the poet offering the images. In short, more is required to alter that portrayal than a varying tradition[75] of Syriac poetry.

Some have attempted to assert the femininity of the Holy Spirit by equating the Spirit with the figure of divine Wisdom in such Old Testament texts as Proverbs 8. That famous text presents a woman, Wisdom, who shares God's eternity and functions as His colleague in the creation of the world. Some of the relevant text of Proverbs 8.22—31 reads:

Yahweh got[76] me at the beginning of His way, before His works of old. From everlasting I was established, from the beginning, from the earliest times of the earth. When there were no depths I was born, when there were no springs abounding with water. Before the mountains

[73]Quoted by Harvey, op. cit., p 125. The penultimate sentence of the quoted text should probably be understood to mean, "Because his breasts were full and it was necessary that his milk not be poured out in vain."

[74]It is of course taken for granted that God is beyond sexuality; I here again distinguish masculinity from maleness.

[75]Even within this tradition the Spirit was portrayed as masculine, possibly to avoid possible misunderstanding as the Syrian church mixed in other churches in the Greco-Roman *oikoumene*. See Harvey, op. cit., 120ff.

[76]The translation of the text has provided difficulty (and even controversy, such as in the days of the debates with the Arians). The word translated above as "got" is the Hebrew *qāna*. Some, such as the Vulgate, Symmachus, Aquila, and Theodotion, translate it as "got, acquired", and this is its normal meaning in the rest of the Book of Proverbs and in the rest of the Old Testament. Others, such as the Septuagint, the Syriac, and the Targums, translate it as "created" (Greek εκτισε). Yet others translate it as "begot" (its apparent meaning in Gen 4.1 and Deut 32.6). Choice between the options is difficult, but we may quote the words of Derek Kidner, in his book, *The Proverbs* (London: Tyndale Press, 1964), p. 80: "This word expresses getting and possessing, in ways that vary with context. Goods are possessed by purchase, children by birth, wisdom—for mortals—by learning. And wisdom for God? … It comes forth from Him; the nearest metaphor is that of birth." Yahweh "got" wisdom in the sense that a couple "has" a child by giving birth.

were settled, before the hills, I was born, before He had yet made the earth, or the first dust of the world. When He established the heavens, I was there. When He inscribed a circle on the face of the deep, when He made firm the heavens above . . . then I was beside Him, as a master workman, and I was daily His delight, rejoicing always before Him, and having my delight in the sons of men.

These verses assert that the origin of wisdom is in God Himself. They speak of wisdom pre-dating the world, and in some measure sharing God's eternity, and say that the Law—Israel's national code—was not simply an arbitrary series of commandments, an expression of human culture, like the codes, laws, and religions of Israel's pagan neighbors. Rather, the Law partook of the attributes of the eternal God, such as His faithfulness, His justice. It was something timeless, transcending all cultures. By personifying the Law's wisdom like this, the passage draws a connecting line from the creative power by which God made the world to the demands of His Law which He gave on Mount Sinai. The lesson is clear: by keeping the Law and heeding the call of ethical wisdom, one participates in and conforms to an eternal norm.

Why personify Wisdom as a woman? It is not simply that the word "wisdom", *hokmah*, is feminine in Hebrew. Nor is it simply that by personifying wisdom as a woman, one can easily apply this feminine image to other ethical contexts, making a contrast between Lady Wisdom and Lady Folly, and offering a moral choice between faithfulness to wisdom and being seduced by "the foreigner who flatters with her words" (see Prov 7.1—8.11). The deification (as it were) of wisdom as God's partner in creating the world seems to require something more, and contains, I suggest, a hidden polemic against the other religions of Israel's neighbors. I suggest that the personification is rooted in the culture of the ancient Near East, in which gods were accompanied by their consorts. Yahweh, as transcendent of the forces of nature, neither has nor needs a consort. In her place, He has His Wisdom. The text uses the thought forms of its day but transforms them in the service of an ethical monotheism.[77]

[77]Bruce Waltke in his work, *The Book of Proverbs*, Chapters 1–15 (Grand Rapids, MI: Eerdmans Publishing Co., 2004), p. 408, suggests that "Solomon invested an Egyptian literary form with Israel's ethical monotheism".

As is well known, Christians have not simply read the passage for its glorification of the Jewish Law. In this poetry, we find Wisdom extolled as the principle by which God made the world. Stoics would later say the same thing about the logos. From this it was a short step to assert that the divine principle of creative design which Solomon praised as the Lady Wisdom, and the Stoics taught as the logos, was in fact the eternal Word of God, made flesh in Jesus Christ. Thus all the Fathers applied this passage, not to the Spirit, but to Christ, gender considerations notwithstanding. Eusebius of Caesarea wrote, "The true and only-begotten Son of the God of the universe . . . is honored in this passage under the name of Wisdom" (*Proof of the Gospel*, 5.1). St Athanasius wrote, "It also says in the Proverbs in the person of Jesus, 'The Lord created me, a beginning of His ways'" (*Statement of Faith*, 3). St Augustine wrote, "According to His form as a slave it was said, 'The Lord created Me in the beginning of His ways'" (*On the Trinity*, 1.12.24). St Ambrose wrote, "Hereby we are brought to understand that the prophecy of the incarnation, 'The Lord created Me in the beginning of His ways' means that the Lord Jesus was created of the Virgin for the redeeming of the Father's works" (*On the Christian Faith*, 3.7.46). St Gregory the Theologian wrote, "The expression ['The Lord created Me at the beginning of His ways'] is used of our Savior Himself, the true Wisdom" (*On the Son, Theological Oration 4*, section 2). Other examples could be multiplied. Suffice to say that the Pauline references to Christ as the Wisdom of God assured a Christological interpretation for this text ever after. The femininity of Wisdom here cannot be used to prove the femininity of the Holy Spirit.

In thinking about the question of the supposed femininity of the Holy Spirit, we may refer again to the usual portrayal of the Spirit in the Old Testament texts that formed the immediate historical context for the Lord's own teaching. It is true, as cited by the Syriac poetic tradition we have been considering, that the word for "spirit" is a feminine noun, and that the Spirit in Genesis 1.2 is said to be "hovering" over the waters of creation, the verb being "used especially of a mother bird hovering over her nestlings."[78] This does not translate into an overwhelming Biblical assertion of the Spirit's femininity, especially since the text in question specifi-

---

[78]Harvey, op. cit., 116. The Hebrew verb is used in Deut 32.11.

cally identifies the Spirit as the "Spirit of Elohim" (Hebrew=*ruah Elohim*), Elohim being a God, not a goddess, and referred to as Yahweh-Elohim later, in Genesis 2.4. More significant are the many references in the Old Testament portraying the Spirit of Yahweh in dramatically masculine or aggressive terms. If femininity is described in terms of "dependence, of receptivity, of communion,"[79] and if "for a man, to live is to conquer, to fight and to kill,"[80] then the Spirit of God is portrayed in the Old Testament in very un-feminine terms: when the Spirit of Yahweh came mightily upon Samson (literally, "rushed upon Samson"), he tore a lion in half as one tears a kid (Judg 14.5–6). At another time, the Spirit came upon him and he went down to Ashkelon and killed thirty of his foes (Judg 14.19).

The experience of someone other than Samson (Samson's general behavior was notably less than exemplary) reveals the same vigor and violence associated with the presence of the Spirit. When the Spirit came upon Saul, he would prophesy (more or less involuntarily; see 1 Sam 10.10, 19.23–24) and "be changed into another man" (1 Sam 10.10). In his first test of kingship, the Spirit came upon him mightily "and he became very angry," cutting up a yoke of oxen in pieces and sending them throughout Israel with the promise, "Whoever does not come out after Saul and Samuel, so shall it be done to his oxen" (1 Sam 11.6–7). Much later in Israel's history, the prophetic word given by the Spirit is described by Jeremiah as "a burning fire, shut up in my bones," which he became "weary of holding in" (Jer 20.9). The Spirit is consistently portrayed in the Old Testament in terms of action and vigor, if not violence. This violent aspect of the Spirit continues into the New Testament: the coming of the Spirit from heaven on the day of Pentecost is with "a noise like a violent, rushing wind," which filled the entire house where the disciples of Christ were seated. The word translated "violent" is the Greek *biaios*, the word used in Exodus 14.21 LXX to describe the *ruah* of God which divided the waters of the Red Sea, and bringing intentional echoes of the *ruah Elohim* which once moved upon the primordial waters of creation. The general Biblical picture of the Spirit is not one of feminine dependence or receptivity, but of virile power and often violent action, and thus does little to justify the characterization

[79]Evdokimov, *The Sacrament of Love*, op. cit., 35.
[80]Evdokimov, *Woman and the Salvation of the World*, 155.

of the Spirit as feminine. More is required to sustain that characterization than Semitic grammar and Syriac poetry.

This masculine portrayal of the Spirit is reflected in creedal formula also. The Niceno-Constantinopolitan Creed describes Him as "the Lord, and the Giver of life"—note: the life-*giver*, not the life-*bearer*, a masculine, not a feminine role. This function of life-giving corresponds to the male rather than the female even in the biological realm. Granted that both genders are involved in the process of procreation, the actual bearing of life devolves upon the woman, not the man. In the binary theological symbolism we are here considering, the masculine *gives* life; the feminine *bears* life. The Divine Spirit is thus masculine, giving life; created nature is thus typologically feminine, "mother nature," bearing life. To ascribe femininity to the Spirit would be to erase this Scriptural typology. We also see this binary typology in the accomplishment of the Incarnation: the birth of Christ was the work of two, for the Creed confesses that He was "incarnate of the Holy Spirit and the Virgin Mary"—the Spirit again fulfilling the masculine role of life-giver, with the Virgin fulfilling the role of life-bearer. The complementary typologies of male and female thus find their echo in the roles played by the Spirit and the Theotokos in the Incarnation, with the Spirit playing the masculine role, not the feminine. Thus, the favored equation of Spirit with feminine cannot be sustained.

The third problem with the feminist approach typified by Evdokimov is the description of holiness as essentially gender-specific. It would seem that men have to transcend their masculinity in their pursuit of sanctity, whereas women have only to accept what they are. Women are pronounced spiritually receptive in their very nature, and more directly connected to the divine Fatherhood, whereas "in a man's nature, there is nothing that corresponds directly to the religious category of fatherhood."[81] For the woman, there is "a mysterious correspondence of the feminine to the divine."[82] It is not simply that the genders are spiritually different, with "the feminine, centered on its own being" and "under the sign of the Nativity and of Pentecost," while "the masculine is energetic" and "under the sign of the Resurrection, of the Transfiguration, and of the

---

[81]Evdokimov, *Woman and the Salvation of the World*, 152.
[82]Ibid., 157.

Parousia."[83] The genders are not simply spiritually different; the woman has the privileged place, and in some sense saves the man by her femininity. As Evdokimov writes, "To the question, 'Will woman save the world?' [the Russian saints such as St Seraphim] would certainly reply, 'Such ministry is implied in her gifts.'"[84]

In this vision, gender is at the heart of human salvation, and the interaction of genders forms the instrument of that salvation. The problem is not with the assertion that men and women are different—a truth acknowledged by all. Obviously men and women have their own modes of interacting with the world and with each other. Men and women each have their own characteristics, with men generally being more prone to action, and women to nurture. These different characteristics mean that men have their own specifically masculine temptations and women their own specifically feminine ones. Detailed elaboration here is hardly necessary; any married person can easily produce a sizable set of lists (usually for the other spouse). But these different modes of being in the world do not translate into different spiritualities, nor are gender differences freighted with spiritual function. Women do not have any secret correspondence with the divine denied to men, and the spiritual realities of the Nativity and Pentecost do not resonate any more with them than they do with men. Men equally with women participate in the saving realities of Christmas, Pentecost, the Transfiguration, and the Resurrection—and on the same terms, namely, repentance and faith.

The Scriptures give no encouragement whatsoever to a privileged view of one gender over another. Indeed, their teaching positively precludes such a view—not least the word of St Paul (favored by feminists) that in Christ there is no male and female (Gal 3.28). This word means that there cannot be a male spirituality different in kind from a female spirituality, or a path to God which is conditioned by gender. Instead, there is the one single spirituality—that of repentance and faith in Christ. To be sure, the challenges inherent in that repentance will differ according to gender—as well as according to age, social status, and matrimonial state. Slaves, for example, will suffer their own specific temptations to offer mere

[83]Ibid., 222.
[84]Ibid., 268.

eye-service, as masters will suffer their specific temptations to treat slaves unfairly, which is why St Paul exhorts both groups individually and in turn with different exhortations (Col 3.22–4.1). Children will have different challenges than will parents; the poor will have different temptations than will the rich. Men and women also suffer different temptations, but these differences of temptation do not imply gender-specific spiritualities. Both genders are exhorted to "put on the panoply of God" (Eph 6.11), and the weapons for this spiritual warfare are same for both men and women. Everyone is hobbled by sin—men, women, rich, poor, slave, free, Jew, Gentile—and no group has any advantage over the other. Paul's refusal to see any advantage with regard to righteousness in being a Jew over being a Gentile (for example in Rom 3.9) translates also into a parity of plight for both genders: both women and men alike stand in equal need of God's help. That is why His grace is poured out on all without distinction. The saving realities of Transfiguration and Pentecost, of the Resurrection and the Parousia, are offered to all alike in the sacramental life of the Church.

Overall then, though the work of Evdokimov and others contains many valuable insights, its understanding of spirituality as rooted in gender represents a significant flaw. It is therefore of limited use in understanding the role of women in the Church.

Conclusion

We have seen in this chapter that the role of women in family and church is rooted in the fundamental, created difference between man and woman, and not in the Fall or a post-lapsarian state. We have characterized this difference as typological. We have observed that the role of the father within the family finds its ecclesial echo and parallel in the role of the pastor within the church, so that the pastor is the father to the church family. This fatherhood of the pastor runs on a different track, and is more fundamental to the church's existence than the ministries of evangelist, prophet, and healer, or the more informal offering of teaching given by laity to those within their social circle. The former requires ordination, while the latter do not. Women and men, despite having different ways of being in world, share the same path to salvation, one not conditioned by gender. Rather, both alike receive the same life from the Spirit of God as they repent and trust in Christ.

We may sum up our conclusions with the words of Brook Herbert, quoting from her essay once again:

> A transfigured ordained priesthood exists solely as love and familial commitment. It is a manifestation of 'fatherhood' constituted and sustained by the Holy Spirit and expressed in the motion of reciprocal love between priest and congregation. Seen in this manner, it is apparent that the role of a male ordained priesthood does not devolve from a negatively conceived resolution to exclude women. Neither does patriarchy reflect a tragic devaluation of female sexuality. Rather, a male priesthood expresses the positive and life-affirming role of fatherhood as an immanent incarnation of Divine Love.[85]

---

[85]Herbert, op. cit., 300.

CHAPTER 5

Deaconesses

The Call for the Revival of the Office of Deaconess

Orthodox women who desire to ordain women to the priesthood often focus discussion on the possible ordination of women to the diaconate, arguing for the revival of the old order of deaconess. This would seem, on the face of it, an excellent place to start the process, since all acknowledge the existence of that order in the early Church. Elisabeth Behr-Sigel opines that "the restoration of the women's diaconate would probably not raise any problem. It existed and flourished during the patristic age. Its restoration is being promoted by such eminent Orthodox theologians as professor Evangelos Theodorou of the theology faculty, University of Athens, and bishop Kallistos of Diokleia in England."[1] As early as the Orthodox women's consultation in Agapia, Romania, in 1976, the call was given to restore the office of deaconess. Behr-Sigel was the keynote speaker. She wrote in her address to that consultation, "The diaconate of women which has fallen into abeyance could be restored if circumstances required it."[2] In the paper from that consultation, "The Concern for Women in the Orthodox Tradition," under the heading, "Proposals: New Roles," Emilianos Timiadis, Metropolitan of Calabria, proposes, "There should be a restoration of the diaconate for women." He also proposes that "more women should be admitted to the Minor Orders, as readers and acolytes."[3] Granted that Orthodox Tradition forbids the ordination of women to the priesthood, what are we to think about this

---

[1]Behr-Sigel, op. cit., 171.

[2]*Orthodox Women: Their Role and Participation in the Orthodox Church* (Geneva: WCC, 1971), 27.

[3]Ibid., 35.

possible ordination of women to the diaconate through the revival of the order of deaconess?

Deaconesses in the Early Church: a Biblical Basis?

In looking at deaconesses in the early Church, it seems that contemporary enthusiasm for the office has overwhelmed historical sobriety. The claim is often made that the office of deaconess is Biblical—i.e., that the Church of the apostolic first century knew the office of deaconess. Thus Behr-Sigel writes, "The roots of this feminine ministry unquestionably go back into the apostolic Church," though she goes on to acknowledge that "it is difficult to be precise about its nature in the first centuries of the Christian era" since "all ministries at that time were fluid and not distinctly defined."[4] Not all are as careful as Behr-Sigel; Topping asserts without qualification that "Phoebe was a deacon. . . . At that time the diaconate was open to women and men on equal terms. The qualifications for both were the same, as were their functions. Later, however, the ministry of the deaconess was restricted."[5] Valerie Karras writes, "In early Christianity and in the Byzantine Church . . . women were fully ordained and ranked as deacons."[6]

Such assertions, however, founder on certain facts, one of which is that there is no conclusive evidence for the existence of deaconesses in the first century. This is implicitly reflected even in the writers who would like to find it there. Behr-Sigel acknowledged that "it is difficult to be precise" about the nature of the early female diaconate. Kyriaki FitzGerald admits regarding the order's early development, "It is difficult to outline the exact historical development of the order of the deaconess."[7] These writers, I submit, find "difficult" the process of tracing the apostolic origin of dea-

---

[4]Behr-Sigel, op. cit., 173.

[5]Topping, op. cit., 118.

[6]Valerie Karras, "Orthodox Theologies of Women and Ordained Ministries," in Aristotle Papanikolaou and Elizabeth H. Prodromou, eds., Thinking Through Faith (Crestwood, NY: St Vladimir's Seminary Press, 2008), 117. She does, however, acknowledge that "their liturgical functions occurred primarily in the private, female spheres of parish life," without apparently seeing how this impacts her prior claim.

[7]Kyriaki FitzGerald, "The Nature and Characteristics of the Order of the Deaconess," in Thomas Hopko, ed., Women and the Priesthood (Crestwood, NY: St Vladimir's Seminary Press, 1999), 94.

conesses, because deaconesses did not then exist. The attempt to establish the existence of the order in the first century focuses upon (1) the figure of Phoebe; and (2) the words of Paul in 1 Timothy (now rehabilitated), where he refers to deacons and then refers to "women likewise" (Greek= *gynaikas hosautōs*) in 1 Timothy 3.11, which is taken by some writers as a reference to women deacons.

The problem with this understanding of these New Testament passages, however, is that if the first century knew an established order of deaconesses, why then do they vanish so utterly and reappear much later, in the third century, where even then they were never universal in the Church as were the other orders of presbyter and deacon? It will not do to attempt to explain this remarkable lacuna by saying "the documents that mention the deaconess are not comprehensive . . . [which] could be said about all the orders in the early church."[8] The fact is that no Church Father refers to deaconesses in these early centuries, though we find reference in Ignatius to bishops, presbyters, deacons, and "virgins who are called widows" (Smyrneans, c. 13), and in the so-called *Apostolic Tradition* of Hippolytus to bishops, presbyters, deacons, widows, readers, virgins and subdeacons. The absence of a single word about women deacons/deaconesses is remarkable if in fact it was of apostolic origin and provenance. The apostolic orders of presbyter/bishop, deacon, and widow (all mentioned in 1 Timothy), spread throughout the world and can thus be easily documented. How did it come about that the ostensibly equally apostolic order of deaconess became instantly invisible after 1 Timothy was penned?

We look first at the celebrated example of Phoebe, mentioned in Romans 16.1–2: "Now I commend to you our sister Phoebe, a *diakonos* of the church in Cenchrea . . . she has been a helper (Greek=*prostatis*) of many and of myself as well." We note first of all that the Greek does not describe her as a "deaconess" (Greek=*diakonissa*), but as a *diakonos*. Her description as *diakonissa* would have justified beyond dispute the translation as "deaconess."[9] Given the use of the word in later liturgical usage (*hē diakon* would eventually be used to designate women deacons/deacon-

[8]FitzGerald, ibid.

[9]The translation adopted by the RSV, the Jerusalem Bible, Phillips, and the margin of the NASB.

esses in the time of Chrysostom), the usage of the term to refer to the office of the female diaconate is not impossible. But it would be exegetically anachronistic to let a later usage of the term determine our translation of the New Testament. More relevant to such translation is the Pauline use of the term *diakonos* in his other writings. In looking at Paul's use of the term, we see that, with the exception of his letter to the Philippians and of the Pastorals,[10] Paul uses the term in the non-technical sense, to denote a servant, not an office-holding "deacon."

Thus a chapter earlier (Rom 15.8–9), Christ is termed a *diakonos* to the circumcision and for the Gentiles, meaning that He serves and fulfills the purposes of God in saving the world. Paul repeatedly describes himself as a *diakonos* (e.g., Eph 3.7; Col 1.23), and further says that he and the other apostles were all simply "*diakonoi* through whom you believed, even as the Lord gave opportunity to each one" (1 Cor 4.5), meaning that they also serve the purposes of God in preaching the gospel. Given the overwhelming usage of *diakonos* as meaning simply "servant" and the strictly-delineated use of the term to designate office-holders in the Pastorals and Philippians, it is unwarranted to assert that the term should be translated "deacon" or "deaconess" in Romans 16.1 in the absence of any other evidence.

What then did Paul mean in describing Phoebe as a *diakonos*? A clue may be found in the further description of her as *prostatis*, a word rendered in the Arndt-Gingrich lexicon as "protectress, patroness, helper." The term is cognate with the verb *proistēmi*, "to rule, direct, manage, care for, give aid." The verb describes the function of ruling in Romans 12.8 and 1 Thessalonians 5.12 (where it refers to the clergy). In describing Phoebe as "a helper of many," a *prostatis pollon*, Paul gives her a title otherwise given to men in authority. The high-priest of Israel, for example, was called the *prostatis tou ethnous*, "the helper of the people."[11] In large cities, the President of the local council was sometimes called *prostatis*—a role elsewhere held by the *archisynagōgos*. This latter title was sometimes bestowed honorifically upon rich and important women.[12] It is difficult

---

[10]Often denied Pauline authorship.

[11]C.C. Ryrie, *The Role of Women in the Church* (Chicago: Moody Press, 1970), 88.

[12]Ryrie (ibid.) writes, "although honorary titles of the synagogue were conferred on

to resist the conclusion, based on the contemporary usage of that time, that the term *prostatis pollon* is an honorific here bestowed on Phoebe as well, since she was performing for the local church the same role as rich patronesses performed for their synagogues. She was therefore a *diakonos*, a servant, in that she had given help (doubtless financial help) "to many," as well as to Paul, and it was in this capacity as patroness of the Church in Cenchrea that she was bearing the letter of Paul to the Romans.

We look next at Paul's words in 1 Timothy 3.8–13:

> [8]Deacons (Greek=*diakonoi*) likewise must be dignified, not double-tongued, not addicted to much wine, not greedy for dishonest gain. [9]They must hold the mystery of the faith with a clear conscience. [10]And let them also be tested first; then let them serve as deacons if they prove themselves blameless. [11]Wives (Greek=*gynaikes*) likewise must be dignified, not slanderers, but sober-minded, faithful in all things. [12]Let deacons each be the husband of one wife (Greek=*gynaikos*), managing their children and their own households well. [13]For those who serve well as deacons gain a good standing for themselves and also great confidence in the faith that is in Christ Jesus."

We have quoted from the English Standard Version, noting translational ambiguities by supplying the Greek. The question is: who are these *gynaikes*—deaconesses/women deacons, or simply the wives of the deacons? We look at the structure of Paul's instructions about *diakonos*, and note a similarity to his instructions about *episcopos* in v. 1–7. That is, in speaking of those doing the work of *episcopē*, Paul sets out certain moral characteristics the candidate must possess, and then speaks of the necessity of the *episcopos* having an orderly household: "He must be one who manages his own household well, keeping his children under control with all dignity" (v. 7). Thus, the fitness of the *episcopos* is reflected in the piety of his family. The same structure is present in discussing the fitness of the *diakonos*: Paul speaks first of the characteristics the candidates must possess ("they must be dignified, not double-tongued . . .") and then speaks of the piety of their families: their "*gynaikes* likewise must be dignified, not

women for outstanding service (usually charity), these titles had no official significance"— i.e., they did not actually rule as the men did.

slanderers . . ."). Paul then goes on to describe the deacons further, saying they must be "husbands of one *gynē*" or wife. If Paul has been discussing male deacons throughout, the passage flows without difficulty, and in parallel with his previous words about the *episcopos*. But if *gynaikes* means "women deacons," the thought is interrupted, for then Paul speaks of male deacons, then female deacons, and then male deacons again, and the parallelism with the previous verses (which speak of the office-holder's family) is compromised. Besides, Paul insists that the deacon must be the "husband of one wife"—if he has just spoken of female deacons as well, should he not add "and the women deacons the wife of one husband"? The best and easiest exegesis would see these *gynaikes* as wives of the deacons.[13] Doubtless these women would have shared their husbands' ministries in the same sense that today a priest's wife shares the ministry of her husband. But this sharing of ministry did not imply ordination for the *gynē*, any more than the practical role of the priest's wife implies her sacramental ordination.

Thus, the New Testament evidence gives no support to the apostolic origins of the deaconess. That being the case, there is no mystery to solve in confronting the absence of the office in the first two centuries. There are no references in the extant patristic literature,[14] because the office did not then exist. The office did not come into existence until the third century, and even then it was not universal.[15] The absence of references to the office until the third century, and its lack of universality even then, are not surprising, but just what we would expect in an office arising in the third century. The later Fathers who had experience of deaconesses in their day (such as Chrysostom, with his friend the deaconess Olympias) obviously would read back this order into the New Testament.[16] But their under-

---

[13]The existence of an Order of Deaconesses in the New Testament would create its own problematic, since such an order would then have vanished from the extant literature for the next two hundred years, as said above. See the following notes.

[14]For references in Origen, see G. Martimort, *Deaconesses: an Historical Study* (San Francisco: Ignatius Press, 1986), 79ff.

[15]Martimort, op. cit., 76ff. See also Manfred Hauke, *Women in the Priesthood?* (San Francisco: Ignatius Press, 1988), 441: "In the Syrian *Didascalia* (middle of the third century), this office is seen as an innovation that requires separate justification."

[16]Ambrosiaster does not seem to have had experience of deaconesses. In his commentary on 1 Tim 3.11, he says, "Paul does not refer here to women deacons, since these are

standable anachronisms do not justify such an anachronistic exegesis for us, and in this case the patristic exegesis of Romans 16.2 and 1 Timothy 3 is not determinative.

What is authoritative in the Fathers, and what should guide us, is their approach, their spirit, their *phronēma*, their fundamental and underlying presuppositions. Their consensus on the fundamentals of the Faith provides the guiding signposts for us today. But their role as spiritual and doctrinal mentors does not extend to offering the fine details of exegesis. For example, we are not bound to reject a Maccabean date for the Book of Daniel because the Fathers did. Fidelity to the Fathers does not reduce contemporary exegesis to mere patristic archaeology. Their doctrinal conclusions about the basics of the Faith set the parameters for our own teaching, but we are permitted to continue a living dialogue about fine exegetical details if we come to possess information they did not have. This involves no logical inconsistency or betrayal of the Fathers. Indeed, the betrayal would be to refuse the task of undertaking rigorous exegesis out of fear.

A further word may be added about a reference in Pliny, who wrote to his master Trajan in AD 112. Pliny was governor of Bithynia, and he wrote to explain his stance about the Christians in his area, saying, "So I thought it the more necessary to inquire into the real truth of the matter by subjecting to torture two female slaves who were called *ministrae*, but I found nothing more than a perverse superstition." The question relevant to us involves the meaning of the Latin *ministrae*—could these have been deaconesses? In asking the question, we note that if one concludes that these *ministrae were* in fact deaconesses, the historical problem noted above remains—namely, how to account for their absence in any of the other extant Christian literature of the time. In fact, it is unlikely that the term *ministrae* refers to deacons/deaconesses. The first thing we note is that these two women were slaves, and this in itself makes it unlikely that they were *diakonoi*, for it was considered problematic for an honorable

not allowed in the church." Concerning this, Hauke writes, "Ambrosiaster was obviously not informed abut the practice of the Eastern Church . . . What he condemns, namely, equivalence between deacons and deaconesses, did not exist there." See Hauke, *Women in the Priesthood?* (San Francisco: Ignatius Press, 1988), 423.

office-holder in the Church to be subject to the whims of pagan masters (compare the later "Apostolic" Canon 82). Gryson suggests they "may be compared to the women associated with deacons in 1 Timothy 3.11."[17] Certainly a term rendered in Latin by a pagan referring to the cries of unfortunate women under torture forms a slender basis on which to assert that the Church of that time knew an order of women *diakonoi*.

Deaconesses in the Early Church: Their Origin and Function

If the office of deaconess did not arise in the first century, when and why did it arise? According to Georges Martimort, in his detailed work *Deaconesses: An Historical Study*, the office arose in the third century mostly in response to felt liturgical needs of the Church—namely, the fact that female candidates were baptized naked (as were all candidates), and that the pre-baptismal anointing of the body required the ministrations of a woman. The deaconess's primary liturgical function was to meet this need. As Martimort said, ". . . the institution of deaconesses lasted only as long as adult baptisms were the norm; the necessity that had brought about its creation was geographically limited and it rapidly became obsolete."[18]

In the *Didascalia*, the original version of which dates to the first half of the third century, in the section "On the Institution of Deacons and Deaconesses," we read:

> "O bishop, you must take for yourself workers for righteousness . . . those among the people who please you . . . should be chosen and instituted as deacons: on the one hand, a man for the administration of the many necessary tasks; on the other hand, a woman for ministry among the women. For there are houses where you may not send deacons, on account of the pagans, but to which you may send deaconesses. And also because the service of a deaconess is required in many other domains. In the first place, when a women goes down into the water, it is necessary that those going down into the water be anointed with the oil of anointing by a deaconess. . . . When the woman who

---

[17]R. Gryson, *The Ministry of Women in the Early Church* (Collegeville, MN: Liturgical Press, 1980), 15.

[18]Martimort, op. cit., 242.

has been baptized comes up out of the water, the deaconess should receive her and instruct and educate her so that the seal of baptism will be preserved."[19]

From this citation we see the work of a deaconess was confined to women, and to situations in which the presence of men would be difficult (such as a man visiting the wife of a pagan), or in situations requiring modesty. The deaconess had no liturgical role in the *synaxis*, and no task regarding the assembled mixed church in general. This explains why the office fell into disuse when adult baptisms became rare and when the Empire was essentially Christian, with no "pagans" left in it. The ministry of the deaconess was limited to working with other women and only in specific situations, unlike the role of male deacon, whose work was with the entire assembled church in the liturgical assembly.

Thus, it was simply not the case that the diaconate was open to women and men on equal terms, with male and female deacons having identical functions. It is true that in this Byzantine period deaconesses (Greek= *diakonissa*) were also called "women deacons" (Greek=*gynē diakon*), or sometimes simply "the deacon" (Greek=*hē diakon*, with *hē* being the Greek feminine definite article). But the offices were quite distinct, and no one seeing male and female deacons function in the church could imagine that it was a single order, equally shared by both sexes. They were obviously completely different ministries. It is true that both were ordained at the altar during the Liturgy itself at the same place, so that their ordering of women deacons was a true ordination and not just a simple blessing.[20] It is true that upon ordination she was clothed in a diaconal *orar*, and that after being given Holy Communion at the ordination Liturgy, she is given the Chalice to hold. But there were other, more substantial differences between male and female *diakonoi*, even in this ordination ritual, and these differences reflect the fact that the male diaconate and the female order of *diakonissa* were two entirely different orders.

For example, the deaconess wore the *orar* differently than did the deacon. (Also, wearing of the *orar* was rapidly becoming customary among

---

[19]Cited in Martimort, op. cit., 38.

[20]This is, of course, still debated, with some seeing the rite being a simple blessing, a *cheirothesia*, and not an actual *cheirotonia*, or ordination.

subdeacons also, so that it being worn by the deaconess does not in itself indicate sacramental parity with the male deacons.) When the female deacon was ordained and given the Chalice, she immediately returned it to the altar, without giving Communion with it, unlike the bestowal of the Chalice to the male deacons, who received it in order to help administer Communion.[21] Also, deacons bowed on one knee for their ordination, resting their heads on the altar; the deaconess stood, and merely inclined her head. Perhaps most significantly of all, the prayers for ordination were entirely different, with the prayer for deaconesses beginning, "O holy and all-powerful God, You who sanctified the female sex . . . " And as Stephen was invoked as the Biblical paradigm for deacons, so Phoebe was invoked for deaconesses.[22] Furthermore, age and marital status differed markedly for male and female deacons. The canonical minimum age for deacons was twenty-five; for deaconesses, it was forty (Quinisext Council, Canon 14). Deacons could be married; deaconesses had to maintain celibacy or be excommunicated (Council of Chalcedon, Canon 15). Taken together, there was no possibility in the Byzantine Church which knew deaconesses of thinking that deaconesses were simply the female version of male deacons. To quote Martimort again, "a deaconess in the Byzantine rite was in no wise a female deacon. She exercised a totally different ministry from that of the deacons."[23]

What then was this ministry? As indicated above in the citation from the *Didascalia*, it was primarily a pastoral service for women. A deaconess was ordained "for ministry among the women," unlike the deacon, who was ordained "for the administration of the many necessary tasks."[24] That is, the sphere of ministry for deaconesses was gender-specific, and deter-

---

[21]This immediate return of the cup in the case of deaconesses, contrasted with the deacons, speaks volumes about the differences between the two orders. She immediately returned the chalice, I suggest, because she had no role in ministering to both genders in the Eucharist, as did the deacon. Unlike his ministry, hers was gender-specific.

[22]See Martimort, op. cit., 146ff. It was natural for the church of that time to invoke the example of Phoebe in speaking of women deacons, given her description in Rom 16.1 as *diakonos*. Its familiarity with deaconesses made such an anachronistic reading of the NT inevitable. But their reading of Rom 16.1 should not determine our own exegesis of the passage, since we have access to scholarly resources which they did not have.

[23]Ibid., 156.

[24]Cited in Martimort, op. cit., 38.

mined by pressing pastoral need. The deacon's sphere of ministry was larger, since he ministered to the entire assembled church, offering the litanies on behalf of all present, giving liturgical directions to all, and helping administer the chalice to all. He had this liturgical role because he was, in fact, the institutionalization of the Church's call to *diakonia*, its service to the needy and poor,[25] so that a church which has no deacon's social ministry is to that degree impaired in its full manifestation to the world of God's redeeming love. That is why the Church has always had deacons, and why the institution and office of deacon began in the first century. (The present reduction of the diaconate to a merely liturgical ornament so that deacons have no real function outside the Liturgy should be redressed. The liturgical work of deacons on Sundays is meant to mirror their pastoral work during the week.) It is otherwise with deaconesses, whose office arose only in the third century. Like the offices of exorcist and door-keeper, the office of deaconess fulfilled a specific function. These offices did not carry the same universal scope of ministry as did the offices of presbyter or deacon but were created to fulfill needs as they arose. That is why these offices eventually ceased to exist when the need for them ceased to exist.

A distinction thus needs to be made between the apostolic offices of bishop/presbyter and deacon on the one hand, and the later pastoral offices of deaconess, exorcist, and door-keeper on the other hand. The former, being apostolic in origin, are part of the Church's Tradition, the deposit which it must guard (cf. 1 Tim 6.20). The Church does not have the freedom to suppress these ministries, since they are apostolic and crucial to the Church's health. The latter, however, are of ecclesiastical creation (like the ancient institutions of the catechumenate and of the energumens, those undergoing instruction and those undergoing exorcism, respectively), and these offices and institutions can lapse or be created according to need. The critical consideration here is not whether deaconesses were ordained or simply blessed in the early Church; it is whether or not the office was part of the apostolic deposit. Since it was not, but was a later creation, questions of whether or not a deaconess was created by *cheirotonia* or *cheirothesia*, by ordination or by blessing, though

---

[25]In Acts 6.1 the Church's "daily distribution of food" to the widows is called daily *diakonia*.

interesting, are ultimately irrelevant to our present discussion. Though the office of deaconess was, I suggest, an office one entered by ordination, it could cease to exist when the Church no longer had pastoral need of it—and so, in fact, it did. The mode of ordination, of whatever kind, proved no impediment to the Church letting the office lapse when it had no further function to fulfill.

Deaconesses Today: A Wise Revival?

We have seen that the Byzantine Church knew, for a while, an order of deaconesses. If such an order existed once, it is possible to revive it again. In this the issue resembles that of reviving a married episcopate: everyone acknowledges that in the early Church, bishops could be married, and that a married episcopate was not canonically prohibited until the Trullan Council in 692. Technically, it is possible to revive a married episcopate (as the Renovationists, a schismatic Russian group under the thumb of the Bolsheviks, attempted in the early twentieth century). The real question for both the issues of a revived married episcopate and a revived office of deaconess is this: is such a revival wise? That is, does it serve the purposes of the gospel and help the Church do its job to the glory of God and the salvation of human souls? In particular, what would be the unintended consequences of such a revival? Could it possibly do more harm than good?

DEACONESSES IN THE COPTIC AND ARMENIAN CHURCHES

In examining this possible revival in the Byzantine Church, we must also look first at the presence of an already functioning order of deaconesses in the non-Byzantine, non-Chalcedonian churches—namely, the deaconesses in the Coptic and Armenian communities. Has their example and experience any relevance for us in the Byzantine or Chalcedonian churches?

The Coptic Church revived an order of deaconesses in the 1980s, (called by them *mukarrasa*, or "dedicated woman"), with the rules for them being finally fixed only in 1992. This is part of a larger revival of female monasticism (a community of active nuns was started in the

1960s).[26] The dedicated women live in small groups under the care of the local bishop, though they are accessible to those they serve.[27] They help their local bishop in social, medical, and educational activities, ministering to women, the elderly, and children. They are not allowed to perform any sacramental tasks, like carrying the Eucharist to the sick or helping the priest baptize, or read liturgically in church.[28] They are dedicated in a new rite recently devised.[29] They dress in distinctive grey ankle-length dress with small grey veils, or secular clothing with a head scarf, and like active nuns are addressed as *tasuni* (i.e., sister). Most take a vow of celibacy before their official dedication.[30] It is thought that there are about six hundred such sisters scattered throughout Egypt (compare the estimate of 485 contemplative nuns for the same area).[31] Many of these women started their monastic career with the intention of becoming contemplative nuns, but were either rejected or advised to pursue their monastic path as an active nun or deaconess.[32] Each day, they must recite the prayers prescribed for all monastics, which distinguishes them from the non-monastic laity.[33]

It is similar in the Armenian Church. In the ninth to eleventh centuries, we encounter "deaconness" as a title for certain nuns. A ritual text from that day, under a rubric that speaks of "ordination of those worthy to be monastics," says that the vesting of nuns should be performed by deaconesses.[34] A church manual of 1184 says that deaconesses are "to preach to women and read the Gospel to obviate a man entering the convent and the nun leaving it."[35] Archbishop Sep'anos Orbēlean of Siwnikʿ, in his

[26]Peternella van Doorn-Harder, *Contemporary Coptic Nuns* (Columbia, SC: University of South Carolina, 1995), 3, 9.

[27]Ibid., 48.

[28]In this they differ from the early deaconesses, whose principal function was to assist the priest in baptizing. Doubtless this difference is accounted for by the fact that adult female candidates for baptism are no longer baptized in the nude.

[29]Ibid., 38. It is significant and a sign of the difference of this order from the ancient order of deaconesses that those ordaining Coptic *mukarrasa* do not simply use the ancient prayers for ordaining deaconesses.

[30]Ibid., 38–39.

[31]Ibid., 36.

[32]Ibid., 85.

[33]Ibid., 145–146.

[34]Oghlukian, *The Deaconess in the Armenian Church*, 14.

[35]Ibid., 15.

History of the Province of Siwnik of 1299, wrote, "There are some women who become deaconesses to preach in nunneries . . . she preaches and reads the Gospel not in the throng on the bema, but on her own in some corner. But let her not approach the service of the holy sacrament in any way like male deacons."[36]

The seventeenth century saw a revival of deaconesses in the monasteries, including in St Catherine's Nunnery, in New Julfa, and in St Stephen's nunnery in Tiflis. Concerning this last convent, we have a letter from the Abbess Yustinianē to the local Armenian bishop, in which she describes the life of nuns in her care. She writes regarding the acceptance and progress of new postulants, "At first we begin gradually to direct her mind towards our monastic path. . . . We continue in this way until we bring her to that perfection whereby she becomes worthy soon to receive the holy office of the protodiaconate."[37] This monastery had eighteen members in 1933, which included twelve deaconesses, ordained for service outside the community.[38] Much of this service consisted of singing at Armenian funerals, an activity that provided much of the convent's financial resources.[39]

In the Armenian Kalfayan community in Istanbul (which came into being in 1866), the nuns were mandated to care for orphans, and the first member of the sisterhood was ordained a deaconess.[40] In 2001, the Catholicos Karekin II of the Armenian Church envisioned the community of nuns then forming in Echmiadzin as a potential source of deaconesses, saying, "The nuns that we will be training will be able to become deaconesses."[41]

This brief survey of the deaconesses in the non-Chalcedonian churches allows us to draw certain conclusions. First, it is apparent that these deaconesses are considered as monastics or part of the Church's monastic life. The Coptic "dedicated women" are akin to "active nuns," they bear the monastic title of "sister," they wear special habits like monastics, and many

[36]Ibid., 15.
[37]Cited in Oghlukian, op. cit., 34.
[38]Ervine, "The Armenian Church's Women Deacons," *St. Nersess Theological Review* 12 (2007): 33.
[39]Ibid., 33.
[40]Ibid., 34.
[41]Ibid., 40.

take vows of celibacy prior to their dedication. The recent creation of this special order, with its own recently devised ordination prayer, must be considered as part of the recent rejuvenation of Coptic monasticism and church life generally. The same monastic character of the office of deaconess is even more apparent in the longer standing institution of Armenian deaconesses, where they classically function as nuns to other nuns within the convent.

Also, we see that the deaconesses within the Coptic and Armenian traditions have entirely different functions from those of the ancient order of deaconess. In the early Church, the deaconess was ordained explicitly to assist the priest in baptizing and carrying the Eucharist to sick women, both situations in which the presence of a male would be pastorally problematic. This sacramental parish function is explicitly denied to the Coptic and Armenian deaconesses. Their role is either largely social (as with the Copts) or largely monastic (as with the Armenians). This distinguishes them dramatically from the deaconesses of the early Church, whose function was largely sacramental.

In sum, the deaconesses of the non-Chalcedonian churches bear little resemblance to those of the early Church, which forms the model and basis for the considered revival of the order today. The current vigor of the order of deaconesses in the Coptic and Armenian churches therefore has little bearing on current discussion of this revival. A successful revival of an order of deaconesses in the non-Chalcedonian churches does not indicate that a revival of deaconesses in the Byzantine Church would meet with similar success, for the Coptic and Armenian deaconesses are clearly not clergy,[42] and the proposed Byzantine deaconesses would be considered clergy.[43]

[42]Compare their explicit ban from helping the priest in any sacramental ministry on the part of the Coptic *mukarrasa*.

[43]The ordained character of the order is stressed by FitzGerald in her essay "The Nature and Characteristics of the Order of Deaconesses," in Thomas Hopko, ed., *Women and the Priesthood* (Crestwood, NY: St Vladimir's Seminary Press, 1999), 108–118.

THE CASE FOR A REVIVED ORDER OF
DEACONESSES IN THE BYZANTINE CHURCH

The current argument for the revival of deaconesses in the Byzantine or Chalcedonian Church is often couched in pastoral terms—there is a need in the parish, it is asserted, for a specifically feminine ministry, such as working with women traumatized by men, for example, victims of rape. Certainly all can see the wisdom in having a woman undertake that delicate ministry. As well, it is sometimes wise to have a woman available to accompany the priest in places where a male priest's presence alone might lead to difficulties. (We are thinking here of situations such as doctors sometimes find themselves in when they examine female patients, and call for a female nurse to stand by as a witness.) For all sorts of reasons (to quote the *Didascalia* ch. 16), the pastor may sometimes want to "take for himself workers for righteousness . . . a woman for ministry among the women."

But there are problems if women are to be ordained as deaconesses for parish work, and I believe these problems make it unwise to proceed with a revival of the female diaconate. I mention three of them.

The first problem concerns the practical lesson taught to the faithful by the sight of women wearing cassocks, being ordained, vested, and communing in the altar—namely, the appearance that women can, in fact, be priests. In my more cynical moments, I often wonder whether this possibility is not the main driving force behind much enthusiasm for the revival of the female diaconate, since whether we intend it or not, this ordination would function as the "thin edge of the wedge." I well recall my own experience in the Anglican Church in North America. In my childhood, Anglicans took for granted a male-only priesthood (I remember a poster advertising for priestly candidates saying in big letters, "It Takes a Man to be a Priest!"—meaning presumably that priests weren't as wimpy as popularly thought). Within a single short generation, the office of deaconess was revived, then the deaconesses were declared (whether they liked it or not; some did not) to be deacons. Women deacons could exist; but women priests—never! Then priests were ordained—but bishops, never! Then auxiliary bishops were ordained, but it was stressed that these did not function as diocesan (or "ruling") bishops. Then diocesan bishops were ordained, and by this time, no dissent was allowed from the new orthodoxy. The "conscience clause" which early in the process allowed one to dissent from the ordination of women was soon declared to apply only to clergy already ordained: new candidates for ordination must acquiesce to women's ordination or be refused themselves. The wedge's thin edge worked very effectively within the Anglican Communion, bringing the faithful from a refusal to ordain women to Holy Orders to popular acceptance of women bishops—and all within a single living generation.

My point here is that what changed popular opinion was not persuasive theological argument, but visual familiarity. The people in the pew by and large did not care about theology or the Bible half so much as about what "felt right" to them. Whatever Bible verses or theology might be thrown about by either side in the debate, the truth was that most Anglican laypeople resisted women clergy at first simply because they had never seen any in Anglican churches. The sight of a woman in a clerical collar or church vestments looked odd, and struck a jarring emotional note, and therefore it must be wrong. They had seen men in all shapes, sizes, and colors in clerical collars and vestments. They had seen boys of varying ages serve as "altar boys." But they had never seen "altar girls" or women priests, and when eventually they did begin to see them appearing in church, the people soon got used to them. The gradual familiarization with the sight of females in vestments wore away the inner emotional resistance to the notion of women clergy. The force of this should be easily understood by any who use icons and know their visual power. It seems obvious, to this writer at least, that the sight of Orthodox women in deaconess's vestments,[44] receiving Holy Communion in the altar with the rest of the clergy, would soon condition the faithful to accept the notion of women priests. One might decry such a development and speak out eloquently of the "need for education of the laity," but the fact remains that people are predisposed to accept what they see portrayed visually before their eyes. It was so for the Anglican Communion, and it would be naive to imagine it would be any different for the Orthodox. Iconically speaking, "seeing is believing."

---

[44]Who knows what these might look like, since clerical vestments have undergone considerable change since the days of St John Chrysostom and deaconess Olympias.

The observation that in the twentieth century the sight of women in cassocks, collars, and vestments led to a widespread acceptance of women clergy highlights the differences between us and the Church in the early centuries. In considering the possible revival of an order of deaconesses such as existed in the fourth century, it is important to realize that there is no such thing as an ecclesiastical time machine, and that we cannot simply turn back the clock. The situation is much different now than it was then. Then, the sight of women deacons vested in an *orar* and receiving Holy Communion in the altar did not lead to an acceptance of women clergy, whereas today such things would. We must ask why this is so.

It is so because of at least two things which separate our situation from that of the fourth century.

The first reason is that the Church of the fourth century experienced a wide variety of ministries. People going to church, especially in large metropolitan centers like Constantinople, saw readers, subdeacons, virgins/ widows, deacons, presbyters, and a bishop, as well as door-keepers and other ministries besides, all sitting or standing in their own established and set areas. None of these was as visually differentiated from the mass of laity by distinct clerical vestments as clergy are now. The faithful of St John Chrysostom's congregation in the fourth century, seeing a woman deacon, would not have concluded that women could also be priests, since those women deacons were obviously simply a part of a well-established order of their own. In today's church, the faithful see usually only one presbyter and perhaps a few altar-boys, all of whom are distinctly vested and distinguished from the laity by these vestments. In Chrysostom's day, there were thus many categories of ordained and blessed service, with deaconesses being only one of them. Today, there are effectively only two categories: clergy and lay, and the existence of deaconesses, being clergy, would inevitably lead to a view that women can be a part of the former.

It is sometimes suggested that the liturgical situation in the Orthodox Church is so different from that of the Anglican Church that the latter's experience of deaconesses leading to women deacons, priests, and bishops cannot properly function as a cautionary tale for the Orthodox. We Orthodox are so familiar with a variety of ministries, all of them different from one another—acolytes, readers, subdeacons—that it is therefore unlikely (the argument goes) that the sight of a vested deaconess in the altar would later lead to women deacons or priests in the altar. It is true, of course, that Orthodoxy still experiences a variety of different ministries, while the Protestant churches such as the Anglican have pretty much collapsed them all into one.[45] But, I would respond, our recognition that these ministries are different from each other[46] pales beside our lack of visual and emotional familiarity with women in the altar—a lack of familiarity often reinforced not only by all but universal custom, but in many cases by citation of canonical precept as well.[47] Orthodox laity—themselves an order in some sense, with chrismation functioning as a kind of ordination—know that readers are different from deacons and priests. But what matters emotionally is not such cerebral knowledge, nor even whether or not the reader wears a particular vestment while reading. What matters emotionally to the mass of the Orthodox faithful is the assigned place of a person during the Liturgy. The sight of a woman standing vested within the altar would utterly overwhelm whatever theology might have been absorbed about the differences between the ministries of reader, subdeacon, and deacon.

This emotional barrier is, I suggest, the real and final barrier to the ordination of women as deacons, priests, and bishops. If one surmounts the emotional trauma of seeing a vested woman deacon in the altar (or emotional oddness, for those less easily traumatized), then no further barrier to other ordinations would long remain. This is not so much a matter of Anglican experience being replicated in the admittedly different liturgical locus of Orthodoxy, as it is the transgressing and outraging of the emotional barriers we Orthodox have ourselves erected in the last hun-

---

[45]For example, the title "Archdeacon" in Anglicanism describes a priest, not a deacon. Deacons seem to have no real function or ecclesial reality. An old story tells of an Anglican priest congratulating his newly ordained deacon with the words, "Congratulations: now you can do everything a layman can!"

[46]But connected—the rite for tonsuring a reader in the Russian church assures the new reader that "the first degree of priesthood is that of reader"—an odd exhortation for one proceeding no further, and one that indeed seems to presuppose that one order leads to another. At the very least the words witness to an understanding, common to all Orthodox churches, that the ministries are considered as parts of a whole.

[47]Canon 44 of the Council of Laodicea. The rationale for the prohibition is debated, and anyway is irrelevant to the discussion here.

dreds of years of liturgical experience. It is true that Anglicans basically have two groups, clergy and lay, while we Orthodox have a number of different ministries. It is also true that one's normal assigned place vis-à-vis the iconostasis divides all Orthodox into two groups. A vested deaconess standing within the altar places her within the ranks of the clergy—on the clerical side of the iconostasis, if you will, with no real barrier to advancing further up the clerical ladder. Theologians may assert all they like that such advancement is not possible, but the Faith is guarded by the mass of the faithful, not by the theologians—as the Patriarchs themselves insisted in their letter to Pope Pius IX in 1848,[48] and the faithful would soon have no defense against or objection to the future ordination of women as priests. One could decry this warning as alarmist; I would suggest that the situation is properly alarming. The assurance "such a thing could not happen in the Orthodox Church" strikes me as savoring of the triumphalism to which we Orthodox are all too often prone. Are our laity so very different from the laity of other churches, or more immune from the creeping secularism that affects so many?

The second and more important difference between our situation and that of the fourth century concerns the recent growth of Christian feminism. In the fourth century, it was taken for granted that a woman, though she could be a deaconess, could never be a presbyter or a bishop. Whether one attributes this mournfully to the patriarchal misogyny of the day, or more cheerfully to a greater respect for Scripture than obtains today, is not the point. The point is that today secular Western culture is preoccupied with the concept of rights in general and women's rights in particular, so that an ideological battle is being fought over the ordination of women. In this climate, the sight of a clerically-vested woman receiving Communion in the altar and being recognized as clergy would send an unmistakable message that would not have been sent in Chrysostom's day.

The second problem with the revival of the office of deaconess is that the desire to ordain deaconesses for ministry in the parish would pay a very poor pastoral return if these were indeed genuine deaconesses. That is, if the Church decided to revive the order of deaconess as it was prac-

---

[48]It reads in part, "Among us . . . the guardian of religion is the very body of the Church, that is the *laos* itself."

ticed in the early Church, complete with an insistence of minimum age requirement and of celibacy, there would be comparatively few candidates presenting themselves in the average parish. There are comparatively few candidates for the male diaconate today, so that in most Orthodox parishes in North America the parish clergy consists entirely of a lone priest, perhaps accompanied by a few altar boys. It is unrealistic to think that many suitable female candidates for the diaconate, possessing the requirements of age and celibacy, would be found. One could dispense, of course, with the canonical age and celibacy requirements, but then one should be honest and cast aside all pretence to be reviving the office of deaconess and simply admit to inventing a new clerical order for women.

Whatever perceived parish needs for ministry to women the revived order of deaconesses was revived to meet, these needs would go unfulfilled, at least by deaconesses. The need for feminine ministry in an overwhelming number of parishes would be met then as it is now—by the priest's wife and by dedicated women in the parish. It remains to be proven that such pastoral needs to traumatized women (such as victims of rape) as cannot be suitably served by male clergy are not in fact being already met by others in the parishes. We have yet to see the proof that this part of parish ministry is broken—why then take the drastic step of introducing a new order of women clergy to fix it? Women workers from the parish can undertake this pastoral task, but they do not require ordination to perform it, and there is no evidence that such ordination would help those receiving it. Indeed, if such women have been hurt by people with authority (husbands, fathers, male partners), it could be the case that the official authority would actually be to the detriment of those ministering. Women from the parish would thus be able to minister most effectively to such people if they did *not* have any official Church authority, but simply reached out as sisters in Christ.

This question of meeting pastoral need throws into high relief one aspect of the debate about the wisdom of reviving a women's diaconate—that of motivation. The office of deaconess was created in the third century to meet a felt pastoral/liturgical need—that of assisting at the baptism of adult women. That need no longer exists, since the vast majority of our baptisms are of infants where nudity is not problematic, or of adults, who now wear clothing of sorts at their baptism. It is reasonable to ask which pressing need would be met by a revived female diaconate. As was said above, there are instances where a feminine presence is required, but those needs are already being met by the women in the parish, apart from ordination. It is difficult to avoid the conclusion that the need that urgently requires satisfying is not a perceived pastoral need in the parish, but the emotional need of female candidates to be ordained.[49] Much of the talk about the Church's need to "recognize and use the gifts of women" boils down to this, since those gifts can be used without ordination.

This observation leads to discussion of a third problem with the revival of the order: that ministry in the parish is often fulfilled by laity, apart from any ordination. The drive to ordain women as clergy so that they can fulfill a ministry undercuts and essentially denies the notion that ministry can be done by laity. This, I suggest, is the real lacuna in parish ministry—not an ordained ministry for women, but a ministry for laity, both men and women. The Church today has too easily accepted the unbiblical notion that ministry involves ordination, so that the clergy are the only ones with ministry—in fact in many places in North America, a clergyman is referred to as "the Minister," as if he were the only one doing worthwhile ministry in the parish. In fact the New Testament is emphatic that ministry is done by all the people of God, laity as well as clergy. All baptized Christians, both men and women, are given gifts of the Holy Spirit at their baptism and chrismation, and are expected to fulfill this ministry. The ministry may be as dramatic as prophecy, or as nondramatic as giving (see Rom 12.6–8), but each member of the Body has a gift and function, and all such gifts and functions are essential if the local Body of Christ is to be healthy and fulfill its corporate calling as the Church of God. One of these ministries is that of deacon (compare Rom 12.7: if one's ministry is *diakonia*, one should fulfill that task "in his serving"). Another may be the feminine ministry of visiting and counselling those women trauma-

---

[49] I suggest that the desire to promote the revival of deaconesses as a route to eventual ordination of women deacons and priests is at the root of the otherwise remarkable lack of attention paid by the proponents of the revival to the modern phenomenon of Coptic and Armenian deaconesses, since these deaconesses are monastic in character and are explicitly differentiated from the clergy. See Mariz Tadros, "The Third Way," *Al-Ahram Weekly Online*, 27 April– 3 May 2000 <http://weekly.ahram.org.eg/2000/479/spec1.htm>.

tized by rape. Whether one's gift involves ordination or not is ultimately irrelevant—what matters is that "to each one is given the manifestation of the Spirit for the common good" (1 Cor 12.7). The urgent need—obscured by the demand for the ordination of women so that they may fulfill their ministry—is the rediscovery and activation of the ministry of every member of the Church.

Those pressing for the ordination of women, either to the diaconate or to the priesthood, speak eloquently of women's spiritual gifts and the Church's need to recognize and use such gifts. They are correct about this need. They are not correct, however, in their unstated and unquestioned assumption that such gifts and ministry require ordination. I believe that the ordination of women deacons would open the door to a catastrophic acceptance of women priests, do nothing to help our parishes fulfill their ministries to the wounded around them, and further entrench the misguided and harmful equation of ministry with ordained ministry. Please be clear: I am not suggesting that the perceived dangers of restoring the office of deaconess somehow "trumps" the Church's need of the restored office. Rather, I suggest that the Church does not now need the restored office at all. The attendant dangers regarding the possible "slide" toward women priests simply make the restoration of deaconesses dangerous as well as unnecessary.

CHAPTER 6

Menstruation and the Communion of Women

*A*fter some thought, I have decided to add this present chapter, since a ban on women's receiving Holy Communion during their monthly times represents the historic practice retained by much of the Orthodox world, not excluding Russia. It also represents the practice of those parts of the North American Orthodox Church which retain this praxis after immigrating to North America. This topic, I would like to stress, has absolutely nothing to do with the previous topics considered in this volume. But since the issue is a live one, one cannot responsibly ignore it. Those taking positions both for and against the historic praxis seem to me to be speaking past one another, with neither of the arguing parties considering in depth the underlying issues, possibly because the issue seems to each party too obvious to require much consideration. Accordingly we will examine the topic at some length here.

The Contemporary Issue

Perhaps few things arouse feminist ire more than the old and customary restrictions placed on women while they are menstruating. These restrictions can include the prohibition against baking prosphora, kissing an icon, getting a blessing from the priest, and entering the nave of the church. (One woman I met in church would not proceed further than the narthex, even though as choir director she sang and directed from the choir loft). All who value such restrictions prohibit women from receiving Holy Communion during their cycle and for forty days after giving birth. After this latter period, the woman must be "churched"—i.e., prayed for by the priest, who asks God to "purify her from all sin and from every uncleanness" and to "wash away her bodily uncleanness and the stains of her soul in the fulfilling of the forty days."[1] She may not enter the church or receive Holy Communion until these prayers are offered.[2]

This custom is deeply ingrained. One teacher at an Orthodox school in North America (he shall remain nameless) advanced the monthly uncleanness of women as the main reason they could not be ordained to the priesthood, since, he said, they could not enter the altar while they were menstruating. In defending this concept of ceremonial or ritual uncleanness (which all admit has nothing to do with sinfulness of soul or any moral failing), reference is usually made to the Old Testament, and to such laws as are found in Leviticus 12. The Theotokos, being a Jewish woman, submitted to the prescriptions of that Law (as we read in Lk 2.22–24), and this is adduced as further evidence of its applicability to Orthodox women today.

These Scriptural references, it is fair to say, do not impress feminists. Topping, for example, refers to the Leviticus law as "written several millennia ago and reflecting primitive taboos based on ignorance." She says that "in view of scientific knowledge of the birth-giving process, we cannot today accept the basic assumption of Leviticus and our Orthodox service . . . this primitive theory of women's 'uncleanness' clearly denigrates Orthodox women."[3] Not surprisingly, appeal is made to Jesus who "simply did not believe in the ritual 'uncleanness' of women."[4] Evdokimov echoes

[1]Department of Religious Education, Orthodox Church in America, *Baptism* (Syosset, NY: Orthodox Church in America, 1972), 27, 29.

[2]Even in Byzantine practice offering such a prayer was not *de rigueur*: as Stuhlman notes in his work, *The Initiatory Process in the Byzantine Tradition* (Piscataway, NJ: Gorgias Press, 2009), the early euchologies found in Codex Barberini (late eighth or early ninth centuries) and in Codex Bessarion (tenth century) contain a prayer for the child first entering the church temple on the fortieth day, but contain no prayer for the purification of the mother. As Stuhlman says, "Later manuscripts add prayers for the purification of the mother on the fortieth day, but these prayers are not found in the early manuscripts" (24). Whatever the church of the ninth century thought regarding the ritual uncleanness of the new mother, it clearly thought that the prayer of the priest was not required for her to become clean.

[3]Topping, op. cit., 126.

[4]Ibid., 120. Topping argues this from Jesus' willingness to touch the woman who was unclean from her flow of blood in Mk 5.25ff. This is a precarious argument: Jesus was also willing to touch the man who was unclean from leprosy in Mk 1.40ff, and yet one should

such sentiments and writes that "in Leviticus . . . woman is viewed as an inferior being, of little value, and without rights."[5]

How are we to regard such a longstanding practice today? For a liturgical fundamentalist, if something is found in our service books, then that settles it, and no change is possible. Longstanding practices are considered de facto to have the approval of the Holy Spirit, and so, because this monthly exclusion of women from the Chalice is longstanding, it is judged authoritative and true. Such longstanding practices, however, include the decline of frequent Communion (for much of the Church's history, the Liturgy was served with few or no lay communicants), and yet many now recognize this to be a deviation from the pure Tradition of the Church. I suggest that a long pedigree is by itself no guarantee of divine approval. As with the previous examinations of the topic of the ordination of women, we need to look to the sources of Orthodox Tradition, to the Scripture and the Fathers.

The Fathers on Women and Holy Communion

Unlike the question of the ordination of women, the Fathers do not speak with one voice on this question, and church councils never examined the issue as they did the issues of the divinity of Christ and the legitimacy of icons. We cannot produce anything like a church consensus on this question based on Scripture and the Fathers. We may therefore regard it as an open question.

Some church voices did declare against the possibility of women receiving Holy Communion during their menstrual periods. (The issue is perhaps further complicated by practical considerations. To put it delicately, modern feminine hygiene products were not then available, and it could be that these considerations bore as much weight with some of the contrary voices as strictly theological considerations.)

---

not conclude from this that He thought leprosy did not make one unclean. Rather, He said to the man, "Go, show yourself to the priest and offer for your cleansing what Moses commanded" (v. 44). Jesus did not exhibit the disdain for the Law and its categories and customs that Topping suggests. Rather, as the Son of God, He was able to transcend these categories.

[5]Evdokimov, *Woman and the Salvation of the World*, 169.

One voice denying women access to the Chalice is that of Dionysius, patriarch of Alexandria. In the year 247, he was asked his opinion by a brother bishop about a pastoral matter. His colleague asks him if women might receive Holy Communion during the time of their menstruation. (The presence of the question shows that and the matter was even then something of a controversy and pastoral dilemma.) Dionysius gives his opinion:

> Concerning menstruous women, whether they ought to enter the temple of God while in such a state, I think it superfluous even to put the question. For I opine, not even they themselves, being faithful and pious, would dare when in this state either to approach the Holy Table or to touch the Body and Blood of Christ . . . if one is not wholly clean both in soul and body, he shall be prevented from coming to the Holy of Holies (quoted in *The Rudder*, p. 718).

Dionysius does not spend much time giving a reason for his opinion. He makes quick reference to the woman with the flow of blood in the Gospel (Mk 5.25ff), saying that as she dared not touch Christ Himself but only the hem of His garment, so the pious should refrain from touching Christ in the Eucharistic Gifts. But one senses that for him it was not really a question. It was, he thought, abundantly self-evident that menstruating women should not commune. The text cited was brought in to support an opinion already arrived at. Though sometimes quoted as a "canon," this ruling is the opinion of but one man answering a letter from a brother bishop.

As we see, Dionysius does not spend much time theologizing. But some of his successors have theologized about the prohibition. The Rev. Lev Puhalo (now Archbishop Lazar Puhalo) wrote, "Menstruation does not render a woman impure or unclean, but it is not 'natural'. It is common to the *fallen nature* not to the *true human nature* in which God created mankind. . . . Menstruation did not enter into the life of Eve whilst she was yet in Eden . . . therefore it is one of the seals of the fall itself. . . . When a woman is menstruating, the former fallen nature is being taught and remembered." The result, for this author, is clear: "The Holy Church, speaking with the voice of the Holy Spirit, has commanded that women not approach the Holy Mystery during their menstruation. . . . To disregard this command is to disregard the Holy Spirit, and it is nothing else but a form of sheer self-worship."[6]

Of greater theological sophistication is the work of Alice C. Linsley. In an interview with *Road to Emmaus* journal, she says,

> "There are two kinds of bloodshed—the bloodshed that pertains to males and the bloodshed that pertains to females, and they are very different. The bloodshed that pertains to men has to do with war, hunting, execution, and animal sacrifice. The bloodshed that has to do with women is menstrual cycle, the blood at intercourse, and the blood at birthing. . . . [These are] binary distinctions so that the blood of women could not be in the same place as the blood pertaining to men. . . . Life and death are opposites. . . . Satan wants to destroy life . . . by blurring all binary distinctions. . . . Human blood and the Blood of Christ cannot be in the same space. This is the most important binary distinction . . . the blood of the female is distinct from the Blood of God. We can't share the same space."[7]

Linsley roots the prohibition in the natural order of religion, with its binary opposites.

Voices prohibiting women from communing during their menstrual periods, however, were not the only voices heard in antiquity. In a Syrian document known to history as the *Didascalia Apostolorum* (or "Teaching of the Apostles") containing anti-Judaic polemics, and dated around the late third century, one reads a contrary opinion. In dealing with this matter, the author says that women may indeed receive Holy Communion during their monthly times "since the Holy Spirit is always in you." The author writes, "Now think about it and recognize that prayer is heard through the Holy Spirit; and the Eucharist is received and consecrated through the Holy Spirit; and the Scriptures are words of the Holy Spirit. Therefore if the Holy Spirit is within you, why do you isolate your soul and not approach the works of the Holy Spirit?" (*Didascalia*,

---

[6] Lev Puhalo, *Synaxis Tracts, No. 4*, "Menstruation and Communion" (Chillwack, BC: Synaxis Press, undated), italics original.

[7] "Stepping into the Stream," *Road to Emmaus Journal* 11.1 (2010): 31–34.

c. 26). His pastoral instruction is that "you shall not separate those who have their period, for even the woman with the issue of blood was not reprimanded when she touched the edge of our Savior's garment; she was rather deemed worthy to receive forgiveness of all her sins. . . . Therefore, beloved, flee and avoid such [legalistic] observances: for you have received release that you should no more bind yourselves and do not load yourselves again with that [yoke of the Jewish Law] which our Lord and Saviour has lifted from you. Do not observe these things, nor think them uncleanness, and do not refrain yourselves on their account, nor seek . . . purification for these things." (Note that the author cites the same passage as did Dionysius of Alexandria, and comes to the opposite conclusion about its significance.)

This eastern opinion was not a unique perspective. In the west, St Gregory the Great (known also as St Gregory the Dialogist) received a letter in 601 from his missionary to Britain, St Augustine of Canterbury (so-called to distinguish him here from St Augustine of Hippo). The missionary asked him whether menstruating women should be allowed to go to church and receive Holy Communion. The bishop of Rome replied:

> "A woman should not be forbidden to go to church. After all, she suffers this involuntarily. She cannot be blamed for that superfluous matter that nature excretes. . . . She is also not to be forbidden to receive Holy Communion at this time. If, however, a woman does not dare to receive, for great trepidation, she should be praised. But if she does receive she should not be judged. Pious people see sin even there, where there is none. Now one often performs innocently that which originates in a sin: when we feel hunger, this occurs innocently. Yet the fact that we experience hunger is the fault of the first man. The menstrual period is no sin; it is, in fact, a purely natural process. But the fact that nature is thus disturbed, that it appears stained even against human will—this is the result of a sin. . . . So if a pious woman reflects upon these things and wishes not to approach Communion, she is to be praised. But again, if she wants to live religiously and receive Communion out of love, one should not stop her."[8]

[8]Epistle 64, To Augustine, Bishop of the Angli.

We see in Gregory's response a recognition of our present condition of the Fall. But (unlike Puhalo) in his view this connection does not require women's exclusion from the Eucharist.

It seems therefore that there were two conflicting approaches to the question in the history of the church. With the decline of frequent Communion for both men and women, the issue increasingly became a moot point, so that the Church never had the opportunity to consider the question with the same thoroughness as it considered Christological questions in the fourth and fifth centuries. The opinion came to prevail that women were unclean during their menstrual times, and that this was an impediment to their receiving Holy Communion. Perhaps the aesthetic and practical difficulties associated with menstruation were the primary cause. But whatever the cause of the completely unofficial consensus, the liturgical prayers in our present service books reflect this development. Yet we still ask: is there a way to judge between the two conflicting approaches? I believe that there is, and that Scripture contains the answer.

The Scriptures on Ritual Uncleanness

THE OLD TESTAMENT APPROACH

The concept of ritual uncleanness is a small part of a larger whole. It was not just menstrual flow or the blood of childbirth that rendered one ceremonially unclean. One was made unclean by touching an animal carcass (Lev 11.24ff), by touching a human corpse (Lev 21.1), or by touching a leper or one with an infectious skin disease (Lev 13–14). A man was made unclean through experiencing a seminal emission (Lev 15.16) or any discharge (Lev 15.1). These various states of uncleanness could also be transmitted through touching something which had come into contact with the source of impurity. If one was to offer sacrifice to God, one had to avoid ritual contamination.

What was the reason for this? This feeling was so deeply held by the ancients that no explanation was deemed necessary in the Old Testament. One suggestion involves the concept of integrity and entirety. Mary Douglas, in her book *Purity and Danger*, surmises that a body which was discharging was seen as temporarily lacking wholeness, and it was this lack that disqualified one from approaching the Divine. It was not that one had done anything ethically wrong for which one needed to repent, but simply that one had not yet recovered the requisite bodily wholeness.[9] Others suggest that the rationale should be sought in the fact that "sinful persons in a fallen death-bound world have been accounted worthy to participate directly in an act of God" (i.e., creation and death).[10] In this view, the presence of blood, semen, and corpses witness to the power of God in bringing life and death, and tactile connection with these realities requires a period of isolation.[11]

Whatever the rationale, this concern for ritual impurity was but one part of a total system of rules regulating one's approach to the Divine. There were other rules as well. In offering sacrifice to commune with the Divine and access divine power and blessing, one had to offer the correct animal—in Mosaic Judaism, animals such as sheep, goats, and bulls, but not swine. One had to offer the sacrifice in the correct way, and in the correct place—using an altar on holy ground, in the place favored and authorized by God, such as in the Temple at Jerusalem. (The Samaritans located the authorized site on Mount Gerizim.) One had to offer the sacrifice through the correct persons—the priests set apart for the task, namely those of the family of Aaron in the tribe of Levi. Certain days were considered more auspicious than others (new moons were favored; compare Is 1.13, 2 Kg 4.23), and some days were regarded as intrinsically more holy than other days (such as the Sabbath days and appointed feast days, such as the Passover). Certain foods could not be eaten, but were regarded as unclean.

All of pagan worship used such concepts as well, with their rigid systems and dichotomies of priest vs lay, holy ground vs profane ground, holy

---

[9]She is followed by Gordon Wenham in his commentary on *Leviticus*, in the New International Commentary on the Old Testament series, ed. R.K. Harrison (Grand Rapids, MI: Eerdmans, 1979), 188.

[10]From the book *Women & Men in the Church*, a study prepared by a Sub-Committee of the Ecumenical Task Force of the Orthodox Church in America (Syosset, NY: Department of Religious Education, Orthodox Church in America, 1980), 42.

[11]I find this view more problematic than the former. If the cause of uncleanness is contact with the power of God, then why does this contact act as a disqualification for offering sacrifice, eating a sacrifice, or contact with the Holy? Should not contact with God's power *qualify* one for experiencing the holy, and not disqualify?

days vs common days, clean foods vs unclean foods, ritual purity vs ritual impurity. Mosaic Judaism was but one of many such religions. Obviously it differed from them in important ways—not the least of which was in its belief in one God. But as far as its cultic categories and dichotomies were concerned, it held to the basic forms of worship found in other world religions.

All of these rules and dichotomies can be summed up in the word *stoicheia*, elementary principles, the A-B-C's of religion. In writing to the formerly pagan Galatians, Paul used this word to describe the fundamental realities of their former religion, as well as the religion of Judaism (see Gal 4.3ff). In Paul's view, "all are in bondage to the *stoicheia*. For Gentiles as much as Jews, this bondage meant adherence to animal sacrifice, the keeping of days, the avoidance of contamination.... Freedom from bondage [to the *stoicheia*] would mean liberation from structures organized by distinctions of holy–profane and clean–unclean, from worries about unclean foods, from distinctions between impure Gentiles and pure Jews, from the fear of contagion."[12]

The ritual impurity of women forms but a small part of this overall system of religion.

OUR MODERN REACTION TO THIS APPROACH

This concept of religion is foreign to us moderns. As heirs of the Enlightenment, we have been trained to regard religion as an internal reality only, as a matter of our ethical behavior. A secularized approach to religion teaches that all that God cares about is whether or not something is sinful or ethically repugnant. This is the only dichotomy that resonates for us—that of right or wrong, ethical or unethical, holy or sinful, and this distinction depends entirely upon our inner disposition. What matters, in this way of thinking, is our mind and its intentions, for our communion with the Divine is the communion of our minds with the Divine Mind.

In this paradigm, such things as bodily integrity, unclean foods, correctly authorized sites for worship, authorized priesthoods, and special authorized days have little significance at all. A dichotomy such as "clean

---

[12]Peter Leithart, *Defending Constantine* (Downers Grove, IL: Inter-Varsity Press, 2010), 325.

food vs unclean food" makes no sense to this paradigm, for how can eating a particular food—such as for example pork—affect our mind and heart and thus affect our relationship with God? A dichotomy such as "holy ground vs common ground" also makes no sense, for we can offer prayer anywhere, and standing in a specific holy location would not affect the quality of our prayer. A dichotomy such as "priest vs lay" makes no sense, for surely anyone can offer a sacrifice or act as a religious functionary, regardless of his ancestry. The requirement that the priest be physically whole (for example, that he not be a eunuch) makes no sense, for such physical states do not touch the inner mind of the person functioning as priest. The dichotomy of "holy day vs common day" makes no sense, for God hears our prayers and accepts our sacrifices based solely on the state of our heart, and whether the day is a Sabbath or new moon makes no difference to that. Finally, the dichotomy "clean vs unclean" makes no sense to this paradigm, for touching a dead body or having a discharge of semen or blood does not change the quality of our prayer, and this quality is all that matters.

This modern paradigm is behind the feminist objection to the Leviticus laws that "this prehistoric taboo" is "based on ignorance and fear of the life-giving process that occurs in the female body."[13] This takes a very narrowed view of ritual uncleanness, ignoring the fact that it was part of a larger whole. (It also takes a very dim view of ancient intelligence: could an agricultural society really have been that ignorant and fearful of the facts of life?) We note, however, the post-Enlightenment presuppositions underlying the objection: menstruation and bodily integrity can have nothing to do with our communion with God, since this communion is entirely a matter of the mind and heart. This may or may not be so, but it needs to be proven, not simply assumed.

All historical religion, pagan as well as Jewish, asserts otherwise. Religion declares that our communion with God involves us in our totality, body as well as spirit, and that our bodily integrity is not irrelevant to our holistic approach to ultimate reality. Other components of religion press forward to make their claims as well—if "we are what we eat," then the foods we ingest form part of the life we offer to God, and the food laws

[13]Topping, ibid., 128.

have some validity. If we live a life defined by calendar and the rhythm of fast and feast, of passing days marked by especially significant intervals (i.e., holy days), then time is also not devoid of religious significance. If physical space can participate in and somehow absorb the presence of God, then the dichotomy of "holy place vs common place" should not be rejected out of hand. In other words, religion with all its *stoicheia* may not be so easily jettisoned by a post-Enlightenment mentality. Bluntly put, from the religious point of view, ritual impurity does indeed disqualify one from communion with God while the condition lasts. The witness of the Old Testament cannot be simply thrown out. It was submitted to by the obediently-Jewish Mother of God, and submission to it was presupposed by Christ as well. It is too facile to say, "Christ himself rejected this Levitical blood taboo."[14] After He cleansed the leper, He commanded him to offer the sacrifice for his cleansing commanded by Moses (Mt 8.4).

THE CHRISTIAN APPROACH TO THE OLD TESTAMENT

Where then does this leave us? In a word, it leaves us with St Paul. Both the example of Christ and the teaching of St Paul show that the effective categories for the Christian are not "right vs wrong," but "new vs old." It is not that the prescriptions of the Law are wrong, but that in Christ a new power has come into the world, one that transcends the old categories, the old and venerable *stoicheia* of the Law.

We see this first in the example and deeds of Christ. Though the Law forbade touching the leper or the menstruating woman lest one contract ritual impurity, Christ touched both and healed them (Mk 1.40ff, 5.25ff). That is, He did not become unclean through them, but rather *they* became clean through *Him*. The piety based on the Law said one could not be pious without fasting, but Christ declared that the joy of His presence superseded the requirements for fasting (Mt 9.15ff), and that this new wine necessitated new wineskins—that is, the newness of the Kingdom necessitated a new approach to piety. Even when Christ healed the leper and commanded that he offer the prescribed sacrifice, He said that the

[14]Topping, Ibid., 128.

sacrifice was primarily "for a testimony to them" (Mt 8.4), for His power was now relativizing the significance of the old Law. The Law led the pious to shrink from entering the house of a Gentile, lest the Jew contract the ritual impurity unavoidable in a Gentile's house, but Christ was prepared to visit the house anyway (Mt 8.7), confident that His power would override this impurity as it overrode the impurity of the menstruating woman. The pious felt the Law required them to wash their hands before eating to remove any possible ceremonial defilement, but Christ declared that real uncleanness came from within the heart—thus again relativizing the old food laws and in effect declaring all foods clean (Mk 7.1ff).

In all of these acts, Christ did not simply abrogate the Law or declare that it was wrong. The situation was more nuanced. The Law was not simply discarded, but the new power of God acting through Christ made the Law and its *stoicheia* no longer final. This is the point of the miracle and lesson in Matthew 17.24ff. In this story, Peter is asked if Jesus pays the two-drachma tax or not. Peter responds to the challenge and impulsively says, "Yes." The tax was required of every Jew, and showed his submission to the Temple authorities whom the tax went to support. Before Peter gets a chance to speak to Christ, Christ speaks to him, and asks, "From whom do the kings of the earth collect tax—from their sons or from strangers?" In other words, kings clearly do not tax their own children, but only their subjects. Christ, as the Son of the Father, is not God's subject, but His Son, and so is not subordinate to the Temple and its authorities as others are. He therefore has no moral need to pay the tax. But, "lest we give offense," He pays the tax, but obtains the money through the miracle of taking the required coin from the mouth of a fish, so that the payment of the tax actually costs Him nothing. In this way, Christ shows that He is not subordinate to the Temple, but that He submits to the Law "lest we give offense" to others. Note the plural "we," for Christ paid the tax for Himself and for Peter. That is, Peter, an image of the Church, shares Christ's exemption from the inner demands of the Law. Disciples of Christ may submit to the *stoicheia* of the Law, but that is only so as not to give offense. The Church participates in Christ's power, and His freedom from the Law.

This approach of Christ finds theological expression in the teaching of St Paul. When Paul reflected upon Christ's salvation and its relationship to the Law, he found the interpretive key in Christ's gift of the Spirit. Christ's death on the cross and His rising from the dead culminated in His ascent to the right hand of the Father and His outpouring of the Holy Spirit (see Acts 2.33). For Paul, it is through the gift of the Spirit that Gentiles now are transformed to receive the blessing promised to Abraham (Gal 3.14). It is through the gift of the Spirit that the old law of sin and death is overcome (Rom 8.2), and that all can become the children of God (Rom 8.15–16). It is through the gift of the Spirit that the old Law, once written on tablets of stone, is now written on human hearts (2 Cor 3.3).

This is because the Holy Spirit brings an experience now of the powers of the age to come. Indeed, the Spirit is a down-payment (Greek= *arrabōn*) of our final inheritance of that age to come (Eph 1.14). He is, one might say, the presence of the future, available now to those who are *en Christō*. As such, the Holy Spirit creates a new reality never before seen in this age—the new humanity, a new birth into a new creation (Jn 3.3–5; 2 Cor 5.17). Formerly, human beings and cultures had been divided into Jew and Gentile. Now there is a new race, neither Jew nor Gentile, for this renewal of old human nature transcends them both. Now there is the possibility of being neither Jew nor Gentile (with their ancient and everlasting mutual hostility), but "one new man" (Eph 2.13–15). In this new humanity, all old rivalries have been transcended—one used to fit into categories such as "Greek and Jew, circumcised and uncircumcised, barbarian, Scythian, slave and free" (Col 3.11), but no more. All those who have been born again and received the renewal of the Spirit belong not to Jews or to Greeks, but to the Church of God (1 Cor 10.32), a people differentiated from Jews and Greeks because they are part of the new creation.

That is why Paul spoke of Christ's being "the end (Greek *telos*) of the Law" (Rom 10.4). Christ was the end of the Law in the sense that He was the *goal* of the Law—the Law had no final and eternal applicability, but was a mere *paidagōgos*, a tutor, a slave whose task it was to bring us to

Christ (Gal 3.24).[15] But Christ was also the end of the Law in the sense of provoking the Law's *cessation*, for now that Christ pours out His Spirit to transform us, the tutor has no more to do (Gal 3.25). In the words of another New Testament writer, Christ "made the first covenant obsolete" and "ready to disappear" (Heb 8.13). A first-century Christian Jew may continue to keep the Law for cultural reasons, but such fidelity to the Law now has nothing to contribute to his salvation and status before God. Now "neither circumcision is anything, nor uncircumcision"—the only thing that matters now is the "new creation" made available through the Spirit of Christ (Gal 6.15). In this new creation, human beings find new possibilities. We can grow into "the knowledge of the Son of God, to a mature man, the measure of the stature of the fullness of Christ" (Eph 4.13). This "mature man" (Greek=*andra teleion*) contrasts with the immaturity of the Law. This was St Paul's point in writing to the Galatians.

The Galatians were tempted to accept circumcision as a necessary part of their status in Christ. They were told by Paul's detractors that they could not worship the Jewish God without becoming Jewish. They had already gone so far as to keep a Jewish calendar, observing "days and months and seasons and years" (Gal 4.10). Paul realized that the truth of the Gospel was at stake, and if they ultimately relied upon circumcision more than on the free mercy and grace of Christ, they would have "been severed from Christ" and "fallen from grace" (Gal 5.4). He therefore wrote his epistle to them to defend his ministry and message and to dissuade them from this catastrophic step.

He did this by revealing the true nature of the Law. It was not of final validity, but only provisional, a tutor to bring Israel to Christ (Gal 3.24). But more than that, the Law had a servile quality. It was well-suited for spiritual infancy and childhood, for a child does not differ much from a slave (Gal 4.1). Children need rules, and the Law could offer only rules. Israel while under the Law was like a slave, in bondage to those rules (Gal 4.3), and those under the Old Covenant could not advance beyond slavery, as Paul strove to show through the allegorical examination of Sarah

---

[15]As Fr Alexander Schmemann writes in *Of Water and the Spirit* (Crestwood, NY: St Vladimir's Seminary Press, 1974), 133: "the old distinction [of the Law] is revealed to be not 'ontological,' but 'pedagogical.'"

and the slave-girl Hagar. To be under the Law, therefore, was to continue in spiritual infancy and slavery (Gal 4.21–25). Christ with His gift of the Spirit brings us to maturity, to sonship, and brings our slavery to an end (Gal 4.4–7). How then could the Galatians think of returning to that state of slavery? The Galatians, though pagans, were under the same bondage as the Jews—that is, bondage to rules, to *stoicheia*, the elementary principles of religion. Now that Christ had set them free from this bondage, how could they think of being enslaved all over again? (Gal 4.8–9).

We see this view of the Law again in Paul's letter to the Colossians. The Colossians were threatened with a form of incipient gnosticism, with its syncretistic mix of Judaism and paganism, which stressed observance of the Law as a precondition of reaching spiritual maturity and salvation. In this system, baptism into Christ was a good beginning, but one needed the Law to achieve full salvation. In response, Paul asserted that Christ was all they needed—faith in Him was not simply the beginning, but the beginning, middle and end. Through faith in Christ, as proclaimed by the apostles "in all creation under heaven" (Col 1.23), they could finally stand before Him "holy and blameless and beyond reproach"—provided that they did not move away from the hope of the gospel proclaimed by Paul and the other apostles (Col 1.22).

In his appeal to the Colossians, Paul showed that the Law has no abiding significance for their salvation. They had to see to it that no one took them captive "according to the tradition of men, according to the *stoicheia* of the world" (Col 2.8). The false teachers courting the Colossians offered the Law, but this was simply a repackaging of religion, the common traditions and religious categories of men, the elementary principles common to religions and cults. They insisted on all sorts of decrees, such as "Do not handle, do not taste, do not touch!" (Col 2.21), a reference to the gnostics' use of the dietary regulations of the Law and categories of clean and unclean. They declared crucial the categories of "food or drink or festival or new moon or Sabbath days" (Col 2.16), but these were not abiding realities. The Law was a mere "shadow," a type, a prophecy. It had no eternal significance. The solidity, the substance, the body (Greek *sōma*) was found only in Christ (Col 2.17). Through Him they died to the *stoicheia* of the world (Col 2.20), to the Law (cf. Rom 7.4). They should therefore reject this gnostic option as an "empty deception" (Col 2.8).

In St Paul's explication of the salvation of Christ through His Spirit, the Law has been demoted to a place of merely national and cultural significance. The Law consists of *stoicheia*, the elementary rules and categories common to all religions, and in the new creation we have transcended these *stoicheia*. Therefore, the religious disqualification of women during their menstrual periods has no relevance to Christians—not because categories of clean-unclean are invalid, but because they form part of religion, and in Christ we transcend religion with all its categories.[16] If the Christian Faith were a religion, these categories would be in force among us. But Christianity is not a religion, and so they are no longer in force. As Fr Alexander Schmemann incessantly taught, "Christianity is in a profound sense the *end of all religion*. . . . Nowhere in the New Testament is Christianity presented as a cult or as a religion. Religion is needed where there is a wall of separation between God and man.[17] But Christ, who is both God and man, has broken down the wall between man and God. He has inaugurated a new life, not a new religion."[18]

Linsley, cited above, makes the case that the blood of females cannot come into contact with sacrificial blood, and she cites the binary distinctions of religion as the reason. Her case against women receiving Holy Communion would be sound, *if* Christianity were a religion, with its system of binary opposites. But we have seen that it is not. Its status as transcending all religion can be seen even in its term for its officiating clergy: clergy are not "priests" (Greek=*iereus*), but "presbyters" (Greek=*presbyteros*) or "overseers" (Greek=*episcopos*). These latter are only called "priests" (a term first attributed to the bishop, not the presbyter) because they preside liturgically at the Eucharistic Sacrifice. Strictly speaking, the Church knows only one true priest—Christ, and His sacrifice on the cross

---

[16]That is why Paul dismisses religious categories of holy day vs common day and clean food vs unclean food as utterly irrelevant in Rom 14, and why he regards all foods to be received with gratitude in 1 Tim 4.3–5.

[17]This in itself explains the abiding concern in all religion to avoid uncleanness, for the rules about uncleanness keep us safe on our side of the wall.

[18]A. Schmemann, *For the Life of the World* (Crestwood, NY: St Vladimir's Seminary Press, 1973), 34.

is our only sacrifice, sacramentally present in the Eucharist. If Christianity were a religion, it would offer sacrifices, and have priests. But it is not a religion, and its presbyters and overseers simply offer an *anamnesis*[19] of the sacrifice of the one true Priest.

Christian women may therefore receive Holy Communion despite what religion would regard as ritual impurity. The defining factor in such an issue is not the dictates of religion, but the presence in us of the Holy Spirit, who makes us a new creation, lifting us all above "the things that are on earth," such as religion. Our aim, whether men or women, is no longer to submit to religious decrees, but rather to "keep seeking the things above, where Christ is, seated at the right hand of God" (Col 2.20, 3.1–2). It is, after all, what the anonymous teacher of the *Didascalia* said, quoted above: "if the Holy Spirit is within you, why do you isolate your soul and not approach the works of the Holy Spirit? . . . Do not load yourselves again with that [yoke of the Jewish Law] which our Lord and Savior has lifted from you."[20]

[19]That is, liturgical memorial.

[20]A document of the Orthodox Church in America in 1980 condemned the barring of menstruating women from Communion. See *Women and Men in the Church: A Study of the Community of Women and Men in the Church* (Syosset, NY: Department of Religious Education, Orthodox Church in America, 1980), 43. See also K. Wehr's "Understanding Ritual Impurity and Sin in the Churching of Women," in *Saint Vladimir's Theological Quarterly* 55.1 (2011): 104.

CONCLUSION

Speaking the Truth in Love

*I*n the preface to this work, I referred to feminism as a Goliath that had come onto the theological battlefield, simply meaning that the issues raised by theological feminism cannot be ignored. This is admitted by many Orthodox writers today, especially in the West. As Behr-Sigel writes, "Rethinking [of the ordination of women] . . . is developing especially in those areas where Orthodox live in direct and permanent contact with Christians of other confessions for whom women priests is a burning issue."[1] The Women's Movement has raised many questions for the Orthodox, and these questions deserve thoughtful and sensible answers. This is admitted by such Orthodox "pillars" as Metropolitan Kallistos Ware and Metropolitan Anthony Bloom.

In his revised classic *The Orthodox Church*, Ware writes, "There is a small but growing minority within Orthodoxy which feels strongly that the whole question [of women's ordination] has yet to receive from Orthodox bishops and theologians the rigorous, searching examination that it requires. . . . [This group] finds the arguments that have so far been advanced, whether against or in favour of such ordination, to be deeply inadequate. . . . There is a mystery here that we have hardly begun to explore."[2] In the revised version of *Women and the Priesthood*, in his article "Man, Woman and the Priesthood of Christ," he further writes, "As yet we are still at the very beginning of our exploration; let us not be too hasty or premature in our judgments."[3]

---

[1]E. Behr-Sigel, op. cit., 170.

[2]Timothy Ware, *The Orthodox Church* (London: Penguin Books, 1993), 293.

[3]Timothy Ware, "Man, Woman and the Priesthood of Christ," in Thomas Hopko, ed., *Women and the Priesthood* (Crestwood, NY: St Vladimir's Seminary Press, 1999), 52.

Metropolitan Anthony writes in the same vein. In the Preface to Behr-Sigel's book cited so often above, *The Ministry of Women in the Church*, Bloom writes, "The Orthodox and Roman Catholics too must rethink the problem of woman in the light of the Scriptures. They must make no hasty statements about her being and her place in the work of salvation. The question of the ordination of women to the priesthood has only recently been asked."[4]

These two pastor-scholars give the impression, and even assert, that the question is an open one. Certainly the question comes to us with a renewed urgency, and it is true that it has yet to receive the authoritative and thoughtful treatment it deserves. But to say this is not to say that the question is a new one, or an open one.

It is not a new one because the Church has already encountered a priesthood which was open to women. It is simply untrue to assert that the reason that the Church never ordained women was because the concept would have been too scandalous to consider in the ancient world. In fact the ancient world was full of priestesses (though Israel, significantly, bucked the trend). And rival Christian confessions also ordained women priests—Epiphanius, as we have seen, writes of the sect of Kollyridians who had women offering a Eucharist. Yet despite having these options available, the Church continued in its primitive refusal to "go and do likewise."

I would further suggest that the question is not really an open one. The Church already knows the answer to the question of whether or not it should ordain priestesses or woman priests, even though it has yet to articulate a full response which deals comprehensively with all that is involved. The Church's experience of Christ (that is, of its Tradition) includes experiences of priesthood and authority, as Christians go to church and live out their lives in their parishes. It also includes experiences of man and woman, of fatherhood and motherhood, as Christians live out their salvation in the ongoing sacrament of marriage in their families. We know what true fatherhood looks like, and true motherhood. We know what godly authority in the Church looks and feels like (and also, sadly, what *ungodly* authority looks like). We know what priesthood is, and how natu-

---

[4]From the Preface to Behr-Sigel's book, *The Ministry of Women in the Church*, xiv.

ral it is to refer to the priest as "Father." This is especially significant, since the title "Father" does not, strictly speaking, denote a priest. If Peter is a priest, his actual title is "Priest Peter"; if a deacon, "Deacon Peter," if a bishop, "Bishop Peter," and these are the designations used by such clergy when they receive Holy Communion. The title "Father" is an honorific, and can be used by non-priests as well, such as monks. The fact that for many of us the title "Father" *means* "priest" reveals much about our experience of priesthood.

Thus the Church has all the pieces with which to articulate a systematic response, but it still needs to assemble them into a coherent whole. To treat the question of women's ordination as an open one is to implicitly deny the significance of our two-millenia long experience of these realities. It is also to say that the Church, through its Fathers, has been reading its own Scriptures wrongly for two millenia about things as basic as man, woman, God, and salvation. In other words, the ordination of women involves a complete denial of our Tradition and of our experience of Christian salvation. Some feminist writers, rigorous and honest thinkers that they are, understand this, and have no problem with rejecting Scripture, Tradition, and Christianity as a whole. For them, the Christian Faith is simply irreclaimably patriarchal, misogynist, oppressive, and wrong, and they (to the credit of their courage and honesty) reject Christianity, preferring either no faith or one of their own making. I stand with them in their relentless honesty: if Church Tradition could be *that* wrong about the basics, then clearly Christ's claim to guide His Church into all truth is mistaken, and the Church has no more access to transcendent divine truth than any other human organization. If that is the case, then why be a Christian? We have, I submit, a clear-cut choice: *either* the Church is guided by the Spirit as regards its basic Faith, *or* it is ultimately at the mercy of its own all-too-human limitations like everybody else. The Orthodox, who claim to be "the Church of the Fathers" and to reverence as holy the Tradition they preserve, are committed to the first of those options. And that precludes the possibility of being wrong about the basics for the first two millenia of its history.

The Church's task, then, is to articulate a full and comprehensive response to all the complex and varied questions raised by feminism. In this, our situation resembles that of the fourth century, when the Church strove to articulate a full and comprehensive response to Arianism. Until that response was given, Christian skirmished with Christian (or Orthodox with Arian, to use our modern labels), arguing sometimes profoundly, sometimes stupidly, always with much "sound and fury," too often "signifying nothing." What was needed was a synthesis of all the material and issues involved, and until this was produced, Arianism continued to gain ground. It was a long battle, for the issues of Christology were complex. Nicea was an important milestone, but the question was not finally settled at Nicea in 325, for the battle continued to rage for the next half century at least. The whole Christological question did not begin to be resolved until the Cappadocian Fathers entered the polemical arena much later. Even then there remained enough to do to keep St Maximus the Confessor busy.

But the point is that the challenge for these Fathers and theologians was not to *discover* the truth about Christ, but to *articulate* it in a comprehensive and convincing way. The truth they already knew. From the days when it confessed, "What was from the beginning, what we have heard, what we have seen with our eyes ... we proclaim to you" (1 Jn 1.1–2), the Church knew the truth about the nature of the Word of the Father. From the late first century, St Ignatius of Antioch was already preaching and writing about "Jesus Christ our God."[5] The Church from its inception knew the truth that Jesus of Nazareth was God incarnate. The challenge was how to *express* it in a way that did justice to the rest of the truths it proclaimed, such as the monarchy of the Father and its monotheistic insistence on one God.

This is the challenge for the Church today: to listen to all the questions and critiques posed by feminist theologians and produce a comprehensive statement of the Church's understanding of men, women, God, priesthood, and salvation. We must listen carefully to what they say and answer clearly. This task requires both humility and courage, for we are tempted either not to listen to unwelcome criticism or else, having listened sympathetically, to give only answers which will not offend.

---

[5]For example, in his letter to the Ephesians.

In all our answers, we must resist the temptation to pretend the question is open when it is not, for God calls us to "guard the deposit," to "contend earnestly for the faith once for all delivered to the saints" (1 Tim 6.20; Jude 3), especially when our answers may be unwelcome.[6] The world, being the world, will of course challenge us, and denounce our practices which are contrary to its own. They denounce us now for not supporting "a woman's right to choose" to abort her baby. They denounce us now for not blessing homosexual unions. None of this should be surprising: the world correctly perceives the Church to be aliens in its midst, and it reacts with the usual xenophobia which has always characterized the world. The denunciations and demands for conformity will not cease until we have conformed. But we must continue to refuse that conformity, for it would betray the Faith given to us by the Lord.

The demand for the ordination of women as priestesses is part of this demand for conformity. That is the true significance of Metropolitan Bloom's admission that "[f]or us Orthodox, the question comes 'from the outside.'"[7] Indeed it does. It comes from the world, and as an expression of the world's partial understanding. Evidence that the demand is rooted in a flawed and partial understanding can be gleaned from the very ones making the demand: the churches (such as the Anglican) which practise the ordination of women, also allow abortion and allow homosexual unions. It is all of a piece. And let us be clear: the demands will not stop once the Orthodox Church has ordained priestesses and women bishops, for the demands have not stopped there for the Anglicans. The world will not be happy until the Church looks and acts like the world. There will be rewards for such conformity, but (not to overstate the matter) they will be confined to this age.

The response to the demands for women's ordination may take some time to be formulated. That is because the issue involves not just the question, "May a woman be ordained to the priesthood?," but also, "What is

---

[6]Certainly the feminists agitating for the ordination of women do not regard it as an open question, and I think it would be folly for the Church to enter into dialogue with them while ourselves treating it as an open question. In this matter, I am reminded of the saying of John F. Kennedy, who is reported to have said, "We cannot negotiate with those who say, 'What's mine is mine and what's yours is negotiable.'"

[7]Behr-Sigel, *The Ministry of Women in the Church*, xiv.

a man? What is a woman? What is a priest? Who is God? What is the authority of Scripture? What is the authority of the Fathers? What is the significance of our collective experience of history?" Arianism involved all these questions, and so does feminism. In responding to the demand for women's ordination, we respond to a complete system of thought, involving many (and often unstated) presuppositions. We must answer our sisters and brothers who ask these questions as fully and clearly as we can, and the truth, as always, must be spoken in love.

List of Books Cited

Behr, John. "The Rational Animal: A Rereading of Gregory of Nyssa's *De hominis opificio.*" *Journal of Early Christian Studies*, vol. 7, no. 2 (Summer 1999): 219–247.

Behr-Sigel, Elisabeth. *The Ministry of Women in the Church.* Redondo Beach, CA: Oakwood Publications, 1991.

Belonick Deborah, (Malacky). *Feminism in Christianity: An Orthodox Christian Perspective*, second edition. Yonkers, NY: St Vladimir's Seminary Press, 2012.

Bobrinskoy, Boris. *The Mystery of the Church: A Course in Orthodox Dogmatic Theology.* Translated by Michael Breck. Yonkers, NY: St Vladimir's Seminary Press, 2012.

Bouteneff, Peter C. *Beginnings: Ancient Christian Readings of the Biblical Creation Narratives.* Grand Rapids, MI: Baker Academic Press, 2008.

Bray, Gerald Lewis. *1–2 Corinthians.* Ancient Christian Commentary on Scripture NT 7. Downers Grove, IL: InterVarsity Press, 1999.

Chesterton, G.K. *The Collected Works of G.K. Chesterton*, vol. 1. Edited by David Dooley. San Francisco: Ignatius Press, 1986.

Clark, Stephen B. *Man and Woman in Christ.* Ann Arbor, MI: Servant Books, 1980.

Cohick, Lynn. *Women in the World of the Earliest Christians.* Grand Rapids, MI: Baker Academic Press, 2009.

Dix, Gregory. *The Shape of the Liturgy.* London: Dacre Press, 1945.

Department of Religious Education, Orthodox Church in America. *Baptism.* Syosset, NY: Orthodox Church in America, 1972.

———. *Women and Men in the Church: A Study of the Community of Women and Men in the Church.* Syosset, NY: Orthodox Church in America, 1980.

Ervine, Roberta. "The Armenian Church's Women Deacons." *St Nersess' Theological Review* 12 (2007): 17–56.

Evdokimov, Paul. *The Sacrament of Love.* Crestwood, NY: St Vladimir's Seminary Press, 1985.

———. *Woman and the Salvation of the World.* Crestwood, NY: St Vladimir's Seminary Press, 1994.

Fee, Gordon. *The First Epistle to the Corinthians*. Grand Rapids, MI: Eerdmans, 1987.

FitzGerald, Kyriaki. "The Nature and Characteristics of the Order of the Deaconess." In *Women and the Priesthood*. Edited by Thomas Hopko, 93–137. Crestwood, NY: St Vladimir's Seminary Press, 1999.

Gorday, Peter. *Colossians, 1–2 Thessalonians, 1–2 Timothy, Titus, Philemon*. Ancient Christian Commentary on Scripture NT 9. Downers Grove, IL: Inter-Varsity Press, 2000.

Gray, John. *Men are from Mars, Women are from Venus*. New York: Harper Collins, 1992.

Green, Michael. *Evangelism in the Early Church*. London: Hodder and Stoughton, 1970.

Gregory of Nyssa, St. *On the Soul and the Resurrection*. Translated by Catherine P. Roth. Popular Patristics Seies 12. Crestwood, NY: St Vladimir's Seminary Press, 1993.

Grosheide, F.W. *Commentary on 1 Corinthians*. Grand Rapids, MI: Eerdmans, 1953.

Gryson, Roger. *The Ministry of Women in the Early Church*. Collegeville, MN: Liturgical Press, 1980.

Guthrie, Donald. *New Testament Introduction*. London: Inter-Varsity Press, 1975.

Hamilton, Victor. *Genesis, Chapters 1–17*. Grand Rapids, MI: Eerdmans, 1990.

Harrison, Nonna Verna. "Orthodox Arguments against the Ordination of Women as Priests." In *Women and the Priesthood*. Edited by Thomas Hopko, 165–187. Crestwood, NY: St Vladimir's Seminary Press, 1999.

Harvey, Susan Ashbrook. "Feminine Imagery for the Divine: The Holy Spirit, the Odes of Solomon and the Early Syriac Tradition." *St Vladimir's Theological Quarterly*, 37.2– 3 (1993): 111–139.

Hauke, Manfred. *Women in the Priesthood?* San Francisco: Ignatius Press, 1988.

Herbert, Brook. "Towards a Recovery of the Theology of Patriarchy." *St. Vladimir's Theological Quarterly* 40.4 (1996): 287–301.

Kallistos of Diokleia. "Man, Woman, and the Priesthood of Christ." In *Women and the Priesthood*. Edited by Thomas Hopko, 5–53. Crestwood, NY: St Vladimir's Seminary Press, 1999.

Leithart, Peter. *Defending Constantine*. Downers Grove, IL: Inter-Varsity Press, 2010.

Lewis, C.S. "Priestesses in the Church?" *God in the Dock*. Edited by Walter Hooper, 234–239. Grand Rapids, MI: 1970.

_____. *The Four Loves*. London: Fontana Books, 1960.

_____. "Membership." In *Fern-seed and Elephants*. Edited by Walter Hooper, 11–25. London: Harper Collins, 1975.

_____. *Reflections on the Psalms*. London: Fontana Books, 1961.

Linsley, Alice. "Stepping into the Stream." *Road to Emmaus Journal* 11.1 (2010): 3–37.

Martimort, Georges. *Deaconesses: an Historical Study*. San Francisco: Ignatius Press, 1986.

Martin, Francis and Evan Smith. *Acts*. Ancient Christian Commentary on Scripture NT 5. Downers Grove, IL: InterVarsity Press, 2006.

Moir, Anne and David Jessel. *Brain Sex*. New York: Bantam, Doubleday, Dell, 1989.

Oghlukian, Abel. *The Deaconess in the Armenian Church*. New Rochelle, NY: St. Nersess' Seminary Press, 1994.

"Orthodox Women: their Role and Participation in the Orthodox Church." Geneva: World Council of Churches, 1977.

Puhalo, Lev. "Menstruation and Communion." *Synaxis Tracts, No. 4*. Chilliwack, BC: Synaxis Press, undated.

Rice, Tamara Talbot. *Everyday Life in Byzantium*. New York: Barnes and Noble, 1967.

Ridderbos, Herman. *Epistle of Paul to the Churches of Galatia*. Grand Rapids, MI: Eerdmans, 1953.

Ryrie, Charles C. *The Role of Women in the Church*. Chicago: Moody Press, 1970.

Schüssler Fiorenza, Elisabeth. *In Memory of Her*. New York: Crossroad Publishing, 1990.

Schmemann, Alexander. *For the Life of the World*. Crestwood, NY: St Vladimir's Seminary Press, 1973.

_____. *Of Water and the Spirit*. Crestwood, NY: St Vladimir's Seminary Press, 1974.

Sommer, Christina Hoff. *Who Stole Feminism?* New York: Simon and Schuster, 1994.

Stewart-Sykes, Alistair. *Hippolytus: On the Apostolic Tradition*. Popular Patristics Series, no. 22. Crestwood: St Vladimir's Seminary Press Press, 2001.

Stuhlman, Byron David. *The Initiatory Process in the Byzantine Tradition*. Piscataway, NJ: Gorgias Press, 2009.

Sub-Committee of the Ecumenical Task Force of the Orthodox Church in America. *Women & Men in the Church*. New York: Department of Religious Studies, Orthodox Church in America, 1980.

Tadros, Mariz. "The Third Way." *Al-Ahram Weekly On-line*, 27 April–3 May 2000, <http://weekly.ahram.org.eg/2000/479/spec1.htm>.

Topping, Eva. *Holy Mothers of Orthodoxy*. Minneapolis, MN: Light and Life Publishing, 1987.

van Doorn-Harder, Peternella. *Contemporary Coptic Nuns.* Columbia, SC: University of South Carolina, 1995.

Waltke, Bruce. *Genesis, a Commentary.* Grand Rapids, MI: Zondervan, 2001.

Walton, John. *Ancient Near Eastern Thought and the Old Testament.* Grand Rapids, MI: Baker Academic Press, 2006.

Wehr, Kathryn. "Understanding Ritual Impurity and Sin in the Churching of Women." *St. Vladimir's Theological Quarterly* 55.1 (2011): 85–105.

Wenham, Gordon. *Leviticus.* New International Commentary on the Old Testament series. Edited by R.K. Harrison. Grand Rapids, MI: Eerdmans, 1979.